# TIME TO GO

## LEAVING EMOTIONAL ABUSE AND OTHER FORMS OF ABUSIVE RELATIONSHIPS

**Your guide on how to leave your abusive spouse quickly and safely even if you have no money**

NORVA SEMOY ABIONA MA, AMABE

Real Fulfilment International

www.MyChoiceMarriage.com

**Time to Go: Leaving Emotional Abuse and other Forms of Abusive Relationships**

First Edition, 2015
Published by Real Fulfilment International
Medway, Kent, England. www.realfulfilment.com

Cover Images©2015 by http://www.dreamstime.com (with permission)

Published in Great Britian

Digital Edition          ISBN 978-0-9931584-1-4

Paperback Edition       ISBN 978-0-9931584-0-7

# TIME TO GO

## LEAVING EMOTIONAL ABUSE
### AND OTHER FORMS OF
## ABUSIVE RELATIONSHIPS

# Dedication

First, I would like to dedicate this book to my wonderful family. To my beloved husband Dr Soji Abiona, my three beautiful daughters Shernorva, Odelia and Jahzeel Abiona. Also to my kind-hearted mother Claudette Ruben, my aunt, Rev. Rosalie Olayokun, my grandmother Eileen Robinson-Murrain, father Rupert John, my uncle, Pastor Mukaila Olayokun thanks for all your advice, help and support.

To Shernorva, you were one of my greatest inspirations for removing us from that abusive environment.

I also dedicate this book to the many people who are in, or were in abusive relationships. Special thanks to Ms Tina Turner, for being one of my inspirations to leave my toxic relationship. To my fallen comrades who didn't make it out alive, like Marcia Henville, Fabiola Ramona Chacon and Anjanie Sammy, but also the ones I did not know. To the individuals still suffering today, I lend my support to your quest for an abuse free existence.

To my heavenly Father, who continues to guide me, I thank you Lord.

# Table of Contents

Acknowledgements ix

Foreword xi

INTRODUCTION 1

CHAPTER 1: Types of Abuse in Relationships 11

CHAPTER 2: Spotlight on Intimate and Combination Abuse 29

CHAPTER 3: Consequences of Abuse 43

CHAPTER 4: Identifying The Signs Behind An Abusive Relationship 55

CHAPTER 5: The Foundations of Abuse 65

CHAPTER 6: How Abusers Continue to Control and Abuse their Victims 77

CHAPTER 7: Deciding Wisely to Leave Your Abusive Spouse 93

CHAPTER 8: Beginning The Thinking and Planning Process 107

CHAPTER 9: Leaving The Abusive Relationship 123

CHAPTER 10: Financing Your Leaving - Even if You Have No Money 139

CHAPTER 11: How Far Should You Go and What if You or Your Family
Own The House? 161

CHAPTER 12: What to Do After You've Left The Abusive Relationship 169

CHAPTER 13: What About Divorce 191

CHAPTER 14: Things to Remember 213

BONUS CHAPTER 219

# Acknowledgements

I would like to express my gratitude to Ms. Claudette Ruben, Mr. Sam Abiona and the woman known as 'iproofread' on fiverr.com for proofreading the book. Thanks to Mrs. Caroline Abiona for your help with my childcare so I could get time to do my research and writing.

Special thanks to Ms. Alicia Lyttle for writing my foreword. I really appreciate your support and advise as I wrote this book.

To all the other individuals who provided support, advice, comfort, read, offered comments, assisted in the editing, proofreading and design, thanks for helping me make this book a reality.

# Foreword

by Alicia Lyttle

"If you fall, fall on your back, because if you can look up you can get up." Those are the famous words said by motivational speaker Les Brown that rang true for me when I left an abusive relationship with nothing... and had to start over. Norva Semoy Abiona understands this too well, having been a victim of domestic abuse as well.

It is from that standpoint, along with a determined passion to help others who have been in similar situations, which has driven Relationship Coach and Speaker, Norva Semoy Abiona, to pen this eye-opening book. Time To Go! is highly in-depth and informative, yet very engaging and refreshing. Norva expertly intertwines her own real-life story with facts, trends and examples of various forms of abuse that exist and how they impact a person – interesting information for all who have encountered abuse in one form or another and those who may not be sure if they are victims. Additionally, her tips for leaving an abusive relationship are so detailed and thorough that they can be seen as highly motivational for any woman (or man) who has long given up the will to leave an abusive partner.

I was really pleased to be asked to write the foreword for this book as it was a chance to get a closer look into the mind of Norva, who has been steadily building a reputation as an inspirational speaker, relationship coach and business owner after escaping from an abusive union. I am confident that readers will consider the information, which was so comprehensively compiled, to be an essential source of information, especially for women who feel trapped in abusive relationships and are not sure what to do to get out.

The extent of the knowledge provided in Time To Go! is such that the reader, whether you are a victim of abuse or the actual abuser, will get a great view of the negative impacts of abuse on family, children, professional life and the wider society. You will find this information in this book highly valuable and will be motivated to follow the actionable steps Norva gives on how to safely and successfully quit an abusive relationship.

Time To Go! is obviously written by a true survivor and serves to be a manual to all those who have had enough and want to make a clean break and start over. It is also a guidebook for people who want to arm themselves with information that will help them identify the early signs of abuse and know what to do if they happen to wind up with an abuser.

As a survivor myself, leaving an abusive relationship was the best decision I ever made. I wish I had Norva's book back then as I would have had more confidence and a guidebook to lead me through those difficult times. Hats off to Norva Semoy Abiona! This book needs to be in the hands of each and every person who needs it.

Alicia Lyttle
CEO: Monetized Marketing
www.alicialyttle.com

# Introduction

*"The mental effect of abuse is deep reaching and can be devastating; it always has an effect on the victim."*

☞ **Author** ☜

When I was a little girl I dreamt of visiting different countries and possibly going to the United Kingdom (UK) to study nursing. Now I have made it my home but it was not under the circumstances I imagined. In October 2000, I boarded a plane with my one year old child and said goodbye to the only place I had called home to that day. I am almost embarrassed to say that I was prepared to give the situation I had left behind a second look. Thank God! That feeling was short lived. People in the UK would ask me, "girl how you could leave beautiful Trinidad to come into this miserable weather?" The answer out my mouth was always 'the educational opportunity'. Yes, that was important to me but the bitter truth was that I wanted to be free. I wanted to live. I didn't want my child to grow up under the hands of an abuser.

I did not feel safe within the population of one million six hundred people. I knew that my effort to leave my abusive husband and more so with our child would have to be done so well that he could never control me again. Any attempt to break free of your abuser or cross their invisible boundary is very dangerous. Not everyone will have to leave for another country or even state but everyone has to be careful to put things in place that will keep them safe of their abusive past.

In all forms of abusive relationships the abuser wants to control you and in many cases keep you to themselves. You are supposed to do everything on their terms and they are not too concerned or affected by your feelings. The use of tactics like isolation, display of power, threats for trivial reasons, unhealthy demands, degradation, pushing the victim to the point of exhaustion, insistence from their distorted perspective and humiliation will most times be accompanied by allowing their victim the occasional indulgence. It can start off gradually or you can be startled by the brazen introduction of an abusive incident. In my case, some methods used included cutting me off from family and friends, controlling my money, physical and sexual violation, wilfully trying to break me emotionally and psychologically. There are instances where some abusers may rationalise their behaviour to the outside world. You may be afraid to tell someone or attempt to leave because you are embarrassed or you believe that if you are found out the abuse will get worse. I felt like I couldn't run or hide. He told me again and again that I shouldn't even try. Armed with his sinister grin he would say, "You're stuck with me! No one else will ever have you! I swear to god that I will find you and kill you!" To make sure that I was in no doubt about just how serious he was, he would look me intensely in my eyes, use his right index finger to make the sign of the cross in his opened left palm then kiss his left palm.

It doesn't matter if you are being hit or not, it's still abuse. Once you are in a relationship with a pattern of being intentionally made unhappy - yes, more than once is a pattern - you are not living as a spouse but serving him according to his set of twisted rules. It is how he says it will be; he is free to do as little or as much as he pleases.

My then husband only wanted me to go where I was permitted to. He would regularly ask me, "where were you?" but when I asked him the same question he would say I was nagging him. For me, it seemed like it meant nothing to him to tell fabricated stories to others about me not cooking, me pestering him and me being with other men. It annoyed him that I was not a big eater because he wanted me to pile on the pounds. In fact he had family, friends and spiritual leaders speak to me about me, "eating like a bird" as he would put it.

The abuser may also attempt to control all your finances. This can sometimes lead them to a dilemma, should I allow them to go to work so we have greater household income or should I keep them at home so I have them even more under my control? Usually the latter wins and the abuser will attempt to get you to either cut back on your hours or leave the job completely.

*One day in an attempt to control and manipulate me on a grand scale my ex husband called in to my work place. I was doing a door to door sales job and the base was approximately one hour fifteen minutes away from my home. My ex was a local police officer at that time, before he chose to leave his job. That morning when I left home we were not on the best of speaking terms. I got into work at about 7am, left the office for my day of sales at approximately 8:30am and returned at around 5:30pm. Now, bear in mind that this was before*

*mobile/cell phones, so it was almost impossible to reach me while I was out the office unless I called in.*

I arrived back at the office and noticed that my boss and some of my senior colleagues looked a bit gloomy. "Norva, how was your day? Come in the office." Now that's a bit strange I thought. "What is it? What's wrong?" I asked in quick succession. "Sit down!" There were four of us in the office, two males facing me and a female by my side. As I sat she put her hand on my shoulder. The manager, Elvis, who was one of the men, stood behind his desk opposite me and said "We got a call from one of your husband's colleagues in the police force. They informed us that he's been shot." My heart raced and tears began to fill my eyes as I let the news sink in. I asked, "How is he? Where is he?" Silence filled the room. "Is he dead?" I asked as I held my face. "We don't know, that's all we were told and then we were asked to relay the message to you." The female beside me gently rubbed my shoulder as she asked me if I was okay. I replied through in between sobs "we weren't speaking this morning. Can I call my mum please?"

I used the office phone and called my mum and asked her if she had heard anything to which she replied no.

My mum's house was a fifteen minute drive away from where I lived. I made the journey to her because my residence had no telephone. I knew that I'd need to call around to get the answers to my questions. While at her house we called the local police station where he worked, the hospital, friends and family who may have had knowledge of the situation, but none of them knew anything at all. We tuned in and listened to the local news but no information about him was forthcoming. I started to get suspicious. I thought that something like this would at least have drawn some attention. After about three hours I left for home.

*When I got in I was surprised to meet my husband cooking. He had a big clean white dressing on his left upper arm. My sadness began to turn into annoyance. "How are you?" He replied "I'm fine!" Then he continued with his cooking. "I heard you were shot today!" I blurted out. "Oh, the bullet grazed me, no big thing!" I looked at the bandage on his arm, "was it here?" I pressed against the spot. He obviously wasn't in pain; instead he gave a silly grin. I told him I was going to get some ice at a friend's house. While there I called my mum and said he's home and okay. I cut the conversation by saying I would talk to her tomorrow. I was too embarrassed to tell her the truth.*

*All night I felt very frustrated, I was thinking about how I was going to face my co-workers the next day. I woke up the next morning and got dressed "Where are you going?" He asked. I replied with a surprised look, "to work." On my way I was rehearsing in my head how I would break the news to my obviously concerned boss and supervisors. I arrived at work and as soon as I stepped into the building I heard, "Norva!" My boss called with a surprised tone, "how are things?" I didn't want to go in his office, which would have led me to blowing my cover of the facade that all was well at home. I walked towards him and said "don't worry he got grazed by a bullet, nothing to write home about. He's doing well." With that I walked away. After a few days my husband removed his bandage and surprise, surprise there was not a mark whatsoever. The entire incident jogged my memory of a time when we were courting. He had pulled a similar stunt but on a smaller scale. I was annoyed then but after this antic I was disgusted and ashamed to mention his lies to anybody.*

What I want you to see in my story is the complexity of what was happening and my ex-husband's manipulative methods of going to any lengths to control me. He, like many other abusers, is what abuse experts label as 'public charmer, private abuser'. They get embarrassment and fear drummed into you so that you will live by their rules.

Now that I have overcome my experience of living through abuse, I am extremely passionate about helping wives live happy and fulfilled lives. As a part of that process, where possible I want to assist those women who are victims of domestic violence safely break free of that relationship. My hope is that through your reading of this book, if you or someone you know is going through abuse you will be able to spot the signs and follow the steps to get away carefully. Traditionally, anyone could second guess you were suffering abuse, except for extreme physical violence. Many victims feel that they will not be taken seriously because they have no proof. I want to dispel these myths and also show you ways to gather evidence to support your case. I will also tell you the importance of formulating a plan for leaving and what to do after you have left, where possible. The thing is that if you attempt to leave without a plan the act of leaving doesn't guarantee an end to the abuse or your safety. It is very difficult if not impossible for you to safely do it all alone, with no guidance or support. I want to empower you to stop pretending that it isn't as bad as it is, and help you come to the conclusion that it's time for it to stop. The mental effect itself is deep reaching and can be devastating. It doesn't really leave your mind, so the sooner you can stop the imprints the better it is for you and those around you, especially when you have children or other dependents involved.

I want you to know that you are wiser, stronger and more deserving of happiness than you can ever imagine. One of my icons is Ms Tina Turner[1]. After watching her true story in the movie 'What's love got to do with it!', I was given an impetus and inspiration to not continue in the domestic abuse that I was living through, albeit more emotional than physical. In a recent video that she shared online[2] she said these very apt words, 'without love and care we cannot survive, without love in action we miss the meaning of life.' The fact that you are reading this book is proof that you know the effort it will take to safely leave the abusive relationship. You have made up your mind to leave and I will help give you guidance as best as I can in these chapters. For that reason I have made the book as fluff free as possible and content rich, with a sprinkling of my own experience, to help encourage and empower you. I have also researched different sources for factual data to help make you aware that you are not alone.

So let's get you started toward an abuse-free life, so that you can experience the true meaning of life, which is a happy and fulfilled living. Leave this abusive existence behind. It's Time To Go!

[1] http://www.biography.com/people/tina-turner-9512276#synopsis
[2] https://vimeo.com/90753535

Key
Principle

Abuse in a relationship is much more common

than previously thought because it shows

up in a myriad of ways.

# I have a very useful gift for you

Firstly, thank you for buying this book here is a bonus gift for you. If you have found yourself trapped in an abusive relationship I want you to successfully leave quickly and safely like I have. Why do I tell you this? Because I want you to know that I understand what you are going through. I am not just someone who studied the topic.

We have all heard about people who tried to leave an abusive relationship but ended up being ridiculed, ostracised, mentally damaged, physically hurt, physically disfigured or even killed. I don't want you to struggle or stress about not knowing what you will need to do before and after you leave. Therefore, it is important that as you embark on this life saving, yet potentially dangerous step to set yourself free that you have a bit of guidance.

This book will go in depth into what you should consider and the things you must do. In addition I have created a **Checklist** for you. You can print it off and have it to hand as you put things in place.

Pick up a copy at: http://www.TheChecklist.MyChoiceMarriage.com

This book and therefore the Checklist will help you get faster, better results than going it alone. The steps work; I have used these steps to help myself and others get out of abuse when it was 'Time To Go!'

Now it's your turn; accept this gift. Get it now!

Blessings and grateful,

*NSAbiona*

**Norva Semoy Abiona** MA, AMABE

CHAPTER 1

# TYPES OF ABUSE IN RELATIONSHIPS

"LOVE doesn't stand for 'Lord Over Very Earnestly™'"

☞ **Author** ☜

**Abuse in various forms that we put up with**

*It was a cool morning and I was sitting on the bed anxiously waiting for him to leave the house so that I could have some time to myself. Actually when he left I would be a free woman for the whole day. The reason being that, every day he would come into the room and tell me how I ruined his life; how I could never walk away from him or he would find me and then kill me.*

*I was getting tired of all this drama, the pulling and shoving of my arm and my chin, being poked with my head completely held back. I was pretending that what was happening was normal and that it was not affecting me.*

*I looked forward to doing the errands I had that day. I knew that while I was out for a while I would escape this madness. I got up from the bed and went over to get my purse. On opening the purse I found that the last $5 I had was gone; and this wasn't the first time this had happened.*

*On the inside I was red with anger, "where's my money? Can you put it back please?" I asked him as nicely as possible. The response I got from him was that what was mine was his. I then asked him how he would feel if I did the same to him. Well actually, I went ahead and did that. I took up his wallet and opened it. As my uncle would put it, 'that's how the fight begun.' He insisted that I should not look inside his wallet not knowing that I had already done so the previous night. His wallet was full of interesting stuff. The kind of stuff that married men should not have.*

*I held onto his wallet tightly and that was my biggest mistake. The pain sliced through my stomach as he thrust his foot into my abdomen. The force pushed me off of the bed onto the hard floor.*

*This was when it hit me that where there is smoke there is fire. People do not act suspiciously without a reason. When they treat you in a manner that is beneath you they are actually covering their tracks. It is at this time that you call a spade a spade and read the signs. Do not remain in that LOVE situation like in my case where the so called love stands for 'Lord Over Very Earnestly™'*

No one plans to enter into an abusive relationship; in fact most people in abusive relationships generally have heard or seen others suffering from abuse and thought to themselves "I would leave him/her right away!" or "I'd never put up with someone treating me like that!". Unfortunately the truth is that abuse in relationships is an all too common occurrence. Whether it's physical abuse, financial abuse, or even emotional abuse, there are millions of victims suffering on a daily basis.

Stereotypically, victims of abuse in relationships are generally women; however victims can be of any gender and any age. Teenagers and young adults make up a vast majority of abuse victims, yet if every act of abuse was reported to the appropriate authorities, the sheer number and range of ages and genders would be astounding. Understanding what abuse really is, how to identify it in others, and determining if you're in an abusive relationship is crucial to your physical and emotional well-being as well as in ensuring that you're in a healthy and cohesive relationship.

If you identify with any of the following, even if it was a minor incident you were abused. If it has happened more than once, yes that is twice or more you are in an abusive relationship.

# What is Abuse?

The very first thought that comes to mind when you say the word abuse is physical violence and it is why many other types of abuse go unreported and unresolved. There are, however, many different types of abuse and many ways that abuse can occur:

### Emotional Abuse

Emotional abuse, unlike some other types of abuse, is harder to detect but it can be just as painful and devastating as the others. This type of abuse can be anything from intimidation to manipulation, or simply criticism and negative comments with an aim to belittle.

Emotional abuse is often used interchangeably with verbal abuse because the emotional pain is frequently caused by verbal attacks. Verbal abuse is a specific type of emotional abuse that is done by the use of the spoken word. Other types of emotional abuse fall under the non-verbal abuse category. For instance, if a husband ignores his wife on purpose when she is physically weak or when she's not able to carry out a task properly or at all, that is emotional abuse. The aim is to emotionally hurt her and make her feel like she is not important. I remember being pregnant and very sick to the point of vomiting a lot. On several occasions I asked my ex husband if he would kindly not spray perfume or cologne in my presence as it was a trigger for my sickness. Furthermore, I pleaded with him, if he would not wear it at all during the period of my pregnancy as it induced nausea. Well, it became a joke to him and he would do it and laugh at what would happen next.

Other examples of non verbal attacks are withholding love or physical touch, leaving you stranded when you go out together or giving you horrible / intimidating looks, all with the intention of making you feel like you don't matter or like you are a bad person. Normally, a combination of both is used by the emotional abuser. In addition, there are instances where victims have become so adapted to the situation that they consider it normal. For some abusers the icing on the cake is when the victim says their maltreatment is not abuse.

Emotional abuse can kill your self esteem!

**Example**: Margaret has been married to her husband Edward for ten years. Since the past one year she has been refusing to touch him or be intimate with him in any way because he has become overweight. She constantly calls him 'fat' and 'ugly' because she hates the way he looks and she wants him to change.

As stated earlier, abuse can happen to men just as easily as it can to women, and it is painful and devastating no matter the gender of the person being abused. In the example, Margret is emotionally abusing her husband by not only refusing to be intimate with him and making him feel rejected but she is also emotionally abusing him by verbally calling him names and insulting him. The emotional damage she is causing is profound and unacceptable.

## Verbal Abuse

Verbal abuse is when someone calls another person names, degrades them either in public or private, spreads rumours in a malicious way, or simply says anything negative to the victim or about the victim to another person. As stated above, verbal abuse is a type of emotional abuse. It can include threats of violence and intimidating statements being said to the victim. The spectrum for verbal abuse is extreme and in more intense cases the victim can actually start believing the lies their partner says. The effect is that it begins to slowly ebb away at your self esteem leading to loss of confidence and self blame for your partner's abusive behaviour.

The verbal abuser enjoys using 'Global Criticism', which are statements and declarations containing misused phrases and words like "always, never, ever, you keep on..., why don't you..., why do you..., I'm fed up of..., do that again and I will..." but it is important to remember that although they are frequently being used the overall statements are usually ploys and seldom based on facts. I mean really, how many people do you know that do the exact thing every single time in a precise way?

> **Example**: Aimee recently went on a break with her long term partner Mark. They both decided they wouldn't see anyone else and would work on getting back together but just needed some time apart. During the split, Mark began spreading rumours about Aimee throughout their friendship groups. These rumours were about how Aimee had an STD and was a horrible mother to their son. Because of this Aimee was outcast from the group and she eventually heard about the rumours and was devastated to think how anyone could feel that way about her.

Verbal abuse doesn't always have to be said directly to the victim. Instead, many abusers in relationships who don't abuse physically do so in very clever ways to hurt their partners. In this example, Aimee's partner Mark was verbally abusive to her when he spread those rumours. He also was emotionally abusive because those comments were negative and damaging to Aimee. When she found out, it actually caused her emotional pain because she was proud to be a mother and was trying really hard. Always watch out for ways in which abusers will hurt their victims because it's not always the bruises and physical wounds that are the only signs!

## Physical Abuse

Physical abuse is the most understood type of abuse because it's fairly straightforward. If someone hits you, spits on you, slaps you, physically hurts or attacks you in any way, then that is abuse. The attacker can sometimes claim it was an 'accident' or that you "made them do it" but don't be fooled. The actions of the abuser are their own, no one else's.

**Example**: James, Jessica's new husband, was furious when he saw that Jessica had accidentally broken something while cleaning. Angry and frustrated he grabbed her arms roughly and pushed her out of the way to see the mess she had made. Jessica had only a slight bruising on her arms but never reported the incident because she wasn't 'hit' by James and because she had made a mess.

Now in this example, James grabbing Jessica's arm is still classified as physical abuse even though he didn't strike her. Any physical violence such as grabbing, slapping, strangling, or even pushing is classed as physical abuse. It should be reported to the authorities even if no 'marks' are left.

When a supposed love relationship ends up being physically abusive one of the repercussions to a victim is inevitably emotional abuse, even when no words are spoken. The physical injury may heal within a short space of time, but emotional abuse leaves you with damaging images and memories.

Physical wounds hurt us on the outside. It may heal naturally and possibly leave a visible scar. In dark skinned individuals it can be more difficult to notice bruises on their skin, therefore our physical abuse can be treated quite easily, less significant as they are.. Sadly, some physical incidents are so severe that victims may end up permanently damaged, disfigured, comatose or dead.

## Abuse of Power

Abuse of power is a very interesting and very widespread type of abuse. It is often found in relationships, especially in couples who have joint assets such as houses, shared bank accounts, children, and more.

When you are in a relationship, the balance of power should be fifty-fifty, however when an abuser is present, that balance will shift dramatically in their favour. The abuse of power in a relationship is where one person uses their so-called position in a way to either be the sole controller or decision maker. This can be over children, money, physical items, the house, car, cell phone, or any other similar thing that can be controlled.

> **Example**: Jeremy lives in South Carolina and had been in a long distance relationship with Linda for two years. They both decided to take their relationship to the next level so Linda moved from her home state of Texas to go live with him. Linda doesn't have a job since she left her old one to be with Jeremy. Additionally, she's low on funds and has saved by moving in with Jeremy since he already had an apartment. One night Jeremy and Linda had a huge argument while they were out for dinner. The argument was over something initially quite small, however tempers flared and Jeremy had had enough. Getting in his car he locked Linda out, rolled down the window and said "Don't bother trying to get in – it's my apartment, my car, my money. Good luck finding your way back to Texas". Linda was devastated and frightened when Jeremy drove off. She frantically called him and a few hours later he came to pick her up and they went back to his apartment and talked it out.

Now, when it comes to abuse of power, the abuser is very aware that they have total control and often will go out of their way to keep control (i.e. not putting their spouse's name on the house or bills). Additionally, when they abuse their power it is often in disagreements to try and gain leverage over the other person and assert their dominance.

## Sexual Abuse

Sexual abuse in relationships consists of any unwanted sexual contact or neglect where the victim has not given consent. A common misconception about romantic relationships is that there is no such thing as rape or sexual abuse in that environment. Fortunately there have been extensive movements to help bring awareness to women and couples about valid consent being given even if a couple is in a committed relationship or even married. Despite all of the efforts gone into raising awareness of sexual abuse in relationships, it still occurs and women are still unaware that it is abuse hence they do not report such incidents to their local authorities.

**Example**: Carrie has been married to Adam for over two years now. They have a lively circle of friends who love socialising. Many of them are still single. The group attend and throw many parties. Both Carrie and Adam drink frequently at these. One night the couple had a small fight while out drinking at a party. They both stayed at the party but drank with their friends instead of together. As the night progressed Carrie became increasingly drunk and was not in full control. Adam, who only drank a few beers, drove them back to their apartment complex where he proceeded to have sex with her.

When Carrie woke the next day she found herself and her husband completely naked in their bed. Confused she couldn't remember anything about the previous night and felt incredibly violated when she realized that he had had sex with her. She knew she would have said no to sex since they were fighting but she never reported the incident to authorities because she loved Adam and because she didn't think it was illegal since they were married.

In the example, Carrie was sexually abused. Being married did not give Adam the right to take advantage of her inebriated state. He sexually abused her and it was a criminal offense. Unfortunately most women never report similar instances because they feel that since they were drunk, or since they are in a relationship, that it doesn't count as sexual abuse. While I was in my abusive marriage I too was sexually abused by my ex-husband and did not report any of the incidents to the authorities nor did I tell anyone. I made threats to him that I would, but never followed through because of ignorance and embarrassment at the time.

Another form of sexual abuse which is not normally viewed as a violation is sexual neglect. A healthy marriage includes sex as a regular part of that relationship; unless there is a reasonable health reason for it not to take place. Even so, a loving couple will find their own ways of mutually expressing sexual intimacy in an agreed, often physical manner. Sexual neglect affects the victim emotionally; it ebbs away at their self-esteem and worth. It is sometimes the case that whilst the abuser denies their partner of sexual intimacy, they may still be meeting their own sexual desires through self-gratification like masturbation, watching pornography, getting sexual pleasure from another person (be it intercourse or otherwise) or even in very extreme cases having sex with animals (also known as bestiality). There are some abusers who simply have no interest in sex and their victim is forced to live in an affectionless relationship. Whether it is because of the demands of work, children, deliberate or outside of their conscious thinking, neglecting to be sexually affectionate to a romantic partner is wrong. This is especially so if this continues despite it being brought to the abuser's attention.

There are some other more frequently used forms of sexual abuse in relationship. These include being humiliated or called insulting names referring to your sexual ability or inability; causing unnecessary sexual pain to a victim during sex; the deliberate refusal to protect the victim from sexually transmitted diseases, infection or unplanned pregnancy; using sexual toys, and other items or objects without the victims consent; and any unwanted sexual pressure or forced activity (including forced/coerced to perform sexual acts or to have sex involving others). All these forms of sexual abuse violate a victim and should simply not be tolerated.

## Stalking

Stalking is a major problem that individuals encounter both in a relationship and outside of one. It is when an individual pursues another or monitors them. It can be done online or in person, and is considered a type of harassment. In relationships, most stalking can occur in the early stages as the abuser works on becoming more and more controlling over their victim, or at the end of the relationship as the abuser tries to keep their connection to the victim. Consider the below example to get a better understanding of stalking and how it progresses in relationships.

> **Example**: Joe was cheated on by a previous wife and now has major trust issues. He began dating Jane and they got married after six months of courtship. Joe has not been able to get the thought of being cheated on out of his head. To help ease his suspicions he takes an alternative route to work every day just to see if Jane is parked outside the salon she works at. On days she's not there he calls her and disguises his questions about her locations by simply asking how she's doing and what she is up to. He constantly is looking to make sure her stories add up with what he is seeing when he checks up on her.

As you can see, Joe doesn't seem to have any malicious intentions when he's 'checking up' on Jane but the harsh reality is that he is actually stalking her. Putting the correct label to his actions is crucial and helps highlight the fact that his behaviour can get worse due to his lack of trust and need to have a constant awareness of Jane's location. If Jane should find out about the stalking, or even give Joe an explanation for her whereabouts when they don't match to what he perceived, this type of abuse can turn from general stalking to emotional abuse, physical abuse, or verbal abuse quite quickly.

The unfortunate truth is that Joe should never have entered into a relationship with previous trust issues. Additionally his actions are abusive towards Jane and he should seek help to correct them so that Jane and he can have a loving and beneficial relationship that they both enjoy.

Abusers can stalk their spouse to make sure that the coast is clear for them to take actions that may not be beneficial or support the relationship. They may also do it to stop their victim from having any type of freedom. I once had a neighbour who showed up, in a taxi, at her husband's place of work every day, at the end of the workday. She did this for over a year, even though she knew her husband absolutely hated it. He felt embarrassed and frustrated, especially because colleagues started making fun of him. He felt powerless in the relationship as she and their children dictated to him what he could and couldn't do. Unfortunately he died at a relatively young age, a very sad lonely married man.

## Financial Abuse

Financial abuse can be a very subtle type of abuse but it is a sign of a much greater problem. It is also often a type of abuse of power, since the idea of dictating how finances are controlled gives the abuser a sense of supremacy and authority.

When you think of financial abuse and relationships, you may immediately think that the abuser is the one who holds control of the money, and you'd be partially right. Actually, financial abuse not only encompasses the control of the money but it also is when one partner tells another that they have an allowance. The abuser tells his victim that they cannot buy (or must buy) something, forces one to have less hours at work, requires that a joint bank account be held, restricts any aid or financial support from outside sources. They can also use their money to have power through the purchase of presents or gifts, and more.

**Example**: Samantha and Carl have two children and receive monthly child support because of the low income bracket they are in. Carl is currently looking for a job. Samantha used to work full time, however Carl soon told Samantha that she should cut down to part time because she was away from home too much and never spent any time with him and the children. Additionally, he also has Samantha pay for his cigarettes and car insurance since he doesn't have any income. Samantha pays because she loves Carl and feels that since they are married with two children that she should make the relationship work for the children's sake. Equally Samantha loves being in a romantic committed relationship and she feels that no other man will be interested in a woman with young children. Unfortunately because Samantha's income was cut, due to her reduced hours plus the fact that she now is home with Carl the majority of the week, he continues to become more controlling over her when they are together.

As you can see, it is sometimes hard to spot financial abuse, however in Samantha's situation, like many other women, it is a very harsh reality that she is dealing with. Just because Carl never took hold of her bank cards or credit cards and told her what she could and couldn't spend money on, doesn't mean he wasn't abusive. Restricting her hours significantly cut her pay. This made it so that she was unable to afford doing activities and other things like she normally would. This kept her at home with Carl more and he was then able to further control her by knowing her whereabouts etc. In a healthy relationship Carl and Samantha would have had a discussion about work and family life balance. They would have then made a decision based on what they see as the best option for them as a family. In the example Carl told Samantha she had to cut down her hours and he didn't give her a chance to express her thoughts and feelings on the matter. This situation has the potential to turn even more highly abusive because Carl is now in a position to further isolate Samantha from the outside world.

## Digital Abuse

With the rise of the internet, a whole new type of abuse has flourished. Digital abuse, or cyber bullying as it is commonly referred to, is a very real and distressing type of abuse that can cause just as much emotional turmoil and trauma as verbal abuse. Teens and adults have become vicious in what is said online, and with social media accounts often open for everyone to see, the spreading of rumours and hurtful statements is done almost instantaneously. Digital abuse is also how many long distance relationships turn sour.

The actual definition of digital abuse in relationships is the use of technologies to harass, stalk, intimidate, or bully a person. This means that digital abuse is when someone uses social media sites to stalk you, uses texting apps on Smartphone to send you hurtful and derogatory messages, or even steals your passwords online to bully and harass you.

**Example**: Andrew and Rae had met through an online dating site. After getting married they continued to use Social Media to share with friends and family how happy they were as a couple. When Andrew and Rae had marital issues Rae made it a point to try to sort the problem out between them as soon as possible. However, Andrew would put up little comments on his Social Media pages which would indicate that the couple were in conflict. Rae absolutely didn't like that practice and she made her feelings on the matter very clear to her husband. One day after a minor incident she checked her Facebook and was startled to see Andrew had sent her a hurtful message while they were both in their living room. Upset she messaged him saying that he should just speak to her directly, especially since they were both at home. Andrew was quick to apologize, saying that he was just venting his frustration. Appalled and angry, Rae turned off her phone and called it a night but left Andrew looking at the television.

The next day Rae's friends on Facebook began messaging her about a detailed post her husband wrote. Andrew had also sent private messages to all of them using her profile. Rae was mortified at what happened and was shocked that the private messages were very revealing about how she felt, her past relationships, and what she wanted in a man. Despite her friends ignoring Andrew's messages, Rae was now embarrassed by what her friends had learnt about her personal life.

Cyber stalking and cyber abuse is all too common especially when people put too much private information online. Unfortunately, cyber abuse doesn't just happen from individuals we do not know or are acquainted with; it can happen from people very close to you like your spouse, as Rae found out. Always be careful about what online practices you engage in because abusers are frequently hurting their victims by exploiting social media sites.

Each of the above mentioned forms of abuse are both dangerous and affects the victim's self-esteem, freedom and right to happiness. Although some are better known than others it does not take away from the fact that each one is unhealthy and should not be imposed on another person. In the next chapter we will look at forms of abuse that are now being brought into public awareness.

Key
Principle

A pattern of hurting you is called Abuse,

no matter which form it shows up as.

CHAPTER 2

# SPOTLIGHT ON

# INTIMATE AND COMBINATION ABUSE

*"The abuser will, over time, keep adding to their*
*artillery of manipulation"*

☞ **Author** ☜

**Nip it in the bud as early as possible**

*The very first time I was physically abused by my then husband was weeks into*
*our marriage. I was in shock and retaliated in an attempt to show that I would*
*not put up with it. I made it clear that I knew he had no right to do that to me.*

*Then it happened two more times within that week. Again, I was bold enough to stand up for myself both verbally and physically. What I did not do was follow through on my promise to make others aware of what he had done. I justified my inaction by telling myself and believing that as I continued to pray, things will change. My thinking at the time was that I didn't want others to hold against him for the rest of his life the fact that he was abusive at the beginning of our marriage. I was planning for our wonderful future and ignoring our miserable unhealthy present.*

*Within a month the pattern was established and he would use phrases like "remember I am a police [officer] so I know the loopholes; you belong to me and I could get rid of you and no one will ever realise." One day as I saw him approaching the house I put on the cassette recorder so I could tape our conversation and his behaviour. But once again I did nothing with it. Because of the threats that I made to tell others about his unloving behaviour, he went ahead of me and started concocting fables which he told my mother, spiritual leaders and other respected elders in my life. I found myself on the back foot, having to defend my character. I was surprised by how swayed some of them were with his lies. They never gave me a chance to say the truth about what actually happened. Honest Norva quickly began to disappear. In her place was Norva the pretender, the fake smile, the happy individual once her husband is not around and the keeping up appearances Norva when her husband was around.*

*One day as he started his pushing and shoving I decided not to fight back. I began to talk to myself in my head. 'Norva, he is bigger and obviously stronger than you are, can you really fight with him?' From that day onwards it took me getting truly enraged to retaliate and when I did he would laugh. In fact, his new approach was to taunt me to see if he could push my buttons. In the process he would sometimes tell me "I will send you mad! I'm Bobby 'The Brain' Heenan." (Wow, until now I never knew where the term came from, now I do thanks to Google and Wikipedia.)*

*The lesson I learnt looking back at those early days is that I should have spoken out and broken my silence as soon as the abuse began. Although the various forms of manipulation and the emotional abuse started first, naively I did not see it for what it was at that time. However, I knew that when the physical violence started, it was definitely wrong.*

*I hope that by reading this and the previous chapters you will identify the abuse you are suffering, if you haven't yet done so. Armed with that knowledge I want to support you in putting an end to this control practice over your life. Let me help you to safely leave the emotional abuse and any other form of abuse that you may be suffering. You deserve happiness and you can have it!*

# Intimate Partner Violence (IPV)

This describes physical, sexual, or psychological harm by a current or former partner or spouse. According to Johnson, M.P. (2006). *Conflict and control: Gender symmetry and asymmetry in domestic violence. Violence Against Women*, there are four types of individual (intimate) partner violence. These are called intimate terrorism, violent resistance, situational couple violence and mutual violent control. They are based on the relationship between a committed couple and the control context of the violence they display. Intimate terrorism is most frequently used by a man against his spouse. He is violent and controlling but his partner is not; later in this chapter I will go a little deeper into this topic. In violent resistance, the individual is violent but not controlling; the partner is the violent and controlling one. In situational couple violence, although the individual is violent towards others, neither the individual nor the partner is violent and controlling towards each other. In mutual

31

violent control, both the individual and the partner are violent and controlling.

## Coercive Control

Coercive control refers to the abuse of a person by violating their human rights and liberty. Many times in the past a woman had to prove that she was physically violated but coercive control does away with that myth. The emphasis is on if an incident is disempowering to a victim; even if it seemed insignificant to anyone else. Women are therefore being given the power to share all incidences of abuse without the dishonour of being asked to show the scars.

The exhaustive list of ways that this type of abuse occurs includes but is not limited to intimidation, humiliation causing fear, physical harm, threats, surveillance, degradation, emotional withdrawal, destruction of property and undermining the victim. Deprivation of social contacts and support, control of resources like money and food, stripping of decision making power and independence, monitoring of time, restricting mobility and transportation and restricted access to communication are also forms of coercive control.

Coercive control is a repeated occurrence of the above mentioned situations, it can be done from a number of different angles, is dynamic and the effects are far reaching socially for the sufferer. They are basically in an imperceptible prison everyday and therefore are not happy.

If you feel like you have to ask your partner for *permission* to make decisions, go to work, speak to certain people, go out with friends, wear certain clothes or makeup or access finances then you may be in a coercively controlled relationship. A number of the methods of

Coercive Control are not seen as an offence on their own. The tactics adopted may pass as part of gendered roles in everyday lives and barely be noticed but its root lies in sexual inequality and discrimination. The practice is wrong and should not be continually tolerated or acceptable.

## Intimate Terrorism

Intimate terrorism (IT) is a severe form of intimate partner violence (IPV) in which violence is one tactic in a general pattern of control of one partner over another partner. The manipulation and violence are designed to get and keep control over the other person in the relationship. The violence may start of as isolated incidents but builds up to being frequent and severe. Over time it may regularly occur at least on a monthly basis, is unlikely to be mutual and is likely to involve serious injury and emotional abuse. Although violence underpins this type of control it is normally used in conjunction with the tactics of non-violent abuse.

The perpetrator of Intimate terrorism is referred to as an Intimate Terrorist. Perpetrators are usually male and their victims are usually female. Some other terms that they may be known as are batterers, abusers, pitbulls and emotionally dependent. Intimate terrorists are desperately attached to their victims; they use violence in order to keep them in the relationship and under their control. In extreme cases intimate terrorists are called "sociopaths" or "cobras". These are even more relentless in their attempt to dominate and control many aspects of them and their partners' lives, including their relationships. Intimate terrorists utilize a combination of several forms of abuse to gain power including emotional, physical, sexual and coercive control.

## Spiritual Abuse

Spiritual abuse refers to when a leader or dominant spouse attempts to use power, control, manipulation, or dominance over another person, in this case their partner, under the guise of being spiritually led by their God or Deity. A spiritually abusive marriage or relationship is a common form of abuse. However, it is not widely spoken about in society unless a story makes the headlines. The vast majority of this type of abuse involves emotional and verbal violation but can also involve other forms of abuse such as physical, sexual, financial, coercion, stalking and many others. The abuser either knowingly, or in some cases unknowingly, persuades the victim that their words and actions are to promote love, honour and respect in the union, when in fact it is a play on the victim's fear by mind control or thought reformation. In other words, the dominant spouse uses religious values, guilt and shame to 'rule and reign over' their spouse.

The abuse in this type of violation is in most cases perpetrated by men over women. Some religious communities teach that the husband has authority over his wife. She is required to submit to the husband in everything. The precepts however, are individually misinterpreted and twisted by some followers to suit their abusive tendencies.

In many cases the victim is subtly lured into being dependent upon the will of the abuser. The fear of being ostracised from, in some cases the only community they belong to, along with factors such as the embarrassment, curses and even the perception of damnation in the afterlife, causes many victims to suffer in silence for much too long. In fact, they may see the abuser as far more influential in their life than any protection offered by law enforcement or the courts. Indeed, many times victims of spiritual abuse find it very difficult to admit that their human rights are being violated, not to mention to share this information with fellow believers or with anyone else for that matter. In extreme cases the victim is willing to stay, even when they know that their life is at risk, as opposed to taking the steps of leaving the abusive situation.

**Example**: Paula had been attending church since the age of three years old and takes her faith very seriously. She was a very outgoing young lady who spent lots of time with her church friends socialising and helping out in her community. She got married to Mark at the age of twenty-two. However, within months her friends started to notice that she was slowly pulling away from them. Mark had actually requested that Paula spent more time with him. He said that would only be for the first year of their marriage and his reasoning was that he loved his wife and wanted to get to know her better.

After 4 years of being man and wife, Paula spends her time either at home doing chores and praying or attending every church service there is during the week. She is now not allowed to speak to her old friends, as Mark was afraid that they could lead her astray. Through attending the weekly women's meeting, Paula made some new friends with wives in the church. She became close friends with two ladies - Janette and Ann Marie. However, within months Mark had requested that she not associate with them as he said 'The Lord' had revealed to him that they don't live their lives strictly by what the scripture teaches. He explained that if she continued to speak with them she will be 'affected by the same evil spirit of defiance' that controls them.

Paula feels lonely as she has no friends except Mark and his parents, they have no children yet and she rarely sees her parents. Her relationship with Mark has become one of subservience; she does what he asks at all times because when she deviated in the past he got very aggressive towards her and excused his reaction with biblical quotations. She is determined to honour her vows to Mark. However, she prays that she will soon be able to do a bit more outside of the home by herself as currently she hardly ventures out if he is not accompanying her.

In the above example Paula seems to be enslaved by her abusive spouse Mark, as opposed to being in a healthy, fulfilling relationship. She, like other victims of spiritually abusive relationships is often made to feel incapable of completing regular tasks without their abuser's help. Furthermore, such individuals may suffer a significant loss of confidence in themselves and are led to believe that they will not be able to function normally without their abuser in their life. What transpires in this type of relationship is that 'being religious' is judged on how obedient and submissive the victim is to the abuser rather than on the promotion of a personal relationship with their God.

In a lot of spiritually abusive relationships the abuser exhibits jealousy and may attempt to isolate their spouse from outside contacts like in the case of Mark and Paula. The natural progression of this type of abuse is that the dominant spouse begins to show disregard for their spouse's privacy, human rights and personal boundaries. Moreover, this private mistreatment of the victim begins slowly to become publicly displayed, as the abuser asserts their authority. If anyone confronts the perpetrator about his or her treatment of their spouse they are greeted with disgust, annoyance and sometime outright ridicule.

Signs of being in a spiritually abusive relationship can include one or a few of the following examples:

- Your spouse is demanding that you submit; remain loyal and obedient to them and all their requests without ever questioning them;
- Your spouse is saying that they heard from God or a spiritual being that they should carry out instructions that are clearly not in your best interests;
- Your spouse uses quotes from religious / spiritual books to justify demeaning you.
- Your spouse is insisting that if you don't do a specific action you will be punished spiritually or even physically.
- Your spouse's general behaviour is like that of a dictatorial leader, where they lord over you rather than show you the love and respect that you deserve.
- Your spouse becomes very uncomfortable or aggressive if you answer back or ask prying questions.
- You live your life full of fear, intimidation and guilt towards your spouse.
- You feel like your spouse controls and manipulate everything you do and say in their presence.
- Your spouse suggests that you are questioning God's authority when you question them.

## Important Risk Factors That Leads to Abuse

An article by the Center for Disease Control and Prevention Services - CDC (online), has highlighted a number of factors that can usually lead to Intimate Partner Violence IPV. The report says that a combination of individual, relational, community, and societal factors contribute to the risk of becoming an IPV victim or perpetrator. They further state that understanding these multilevel factors can help identify various opportunities for prevention. I also believe that with this knowledge it makes us better able to help victims as they seek to break free from their abuser.

The following is their long list of categorised risk factors for IPV:-

*Individual Risk Factors*

- Low self-esteem

- Low income

- Low academic achievement

- Young age

- Aggressive or delinquent behaviour as a youth

- Heavy alcohol and drug use

- Depression

- Anger and hostility

- Antisocial personality traits

- Borderline personality traits

- Prior history of being physically abusive

- Having few friends and being isolated from other people

- Unemployment

- Emotional dependence and insecurity

- Belief in strict gender roles (e.g., male dominance and aggression in relationships)

- Desire for power and control in relationships

- Perpetrating psychological aggression

- Being a victim of physical or psychological abuse (consistently one of the strongest predictors of perpetration)

- History of experiencing poor parenting as a child

- History of experiencing physical discipline as a child

*Relationship Factors*

- Marital conflict-fights, tension, and other struggles

- Marital instability-divorces or separations

- Dominance and control of the relationship by one partner over the other

- Economic stress

- Unhealthy family relationships and interactions

*Community Factors*

- Poverty and associated factors (e.g., overcrowding)

- Low social capital-lack of institutions, relationships, and norms that shape a community's social interactions

- Weak community sanctions against IPV (e.g., unwillingness of neighbours to intervene in situations where they witness violence)

*Societal Factors*

- Traditional gender norms (e.g., women should stay at home, not enter workforce, and be submissive; men support the family and make the decisions)

Source: U.S. Department of Health and Human - Center for Disease Control and Prevention CDC (online)

Research last updated: February 11, 2015

http://www.cdc.gov/violenceprevention/intimatepartnerviolence/riskpr otectivefactors.html

In order to be able to take any step toward freedom from an abusive relationship the victim first has to stop being over concerned about the thoughts and actions of others. They will have to start looking inwardly, to figure out what would help them be able to live a happy and mentally healthy life.

Key
Principle

Often times an abuser will use a combination

of different forms of abuse to

lord over their victim.

CHAPTER 3

# CONSEQUENCES OF ABUSE

*"An abused parent inadvertently has abused children."*

☞ **Author** ☜

## Winding me up using the baby

*After five years of marriage and abuse, I gave birth to my daughter. Her birth brought a new sense of joy and purpose to my life and also meant that I began to take more of a microscopic look at the environment I was allowing her to live in. One day as I cooked in the open-plan kitchen, I watched as my ex-husband sat in the living room with the baby. Our eyes made contact, and I felt like he gave me one of those looks that said, 'watch what I'm about to do'. I stopped what I was doing and in a clandestine manner I looked on with anticipation. He had a pattern of doing things to wind me up; this was more of a daily occurrence, so I was in the habit of grinning and bearing on a very regular basis.*

*That day I watched as he repeatedly put the baby's thumb in her mouth, even though she was initially not interested in having it there. Now, during my pregnancy and even after giving birth I had spoken over and over again to him and others about how much I didn't want this baby, or any other children I would give birth to in the future, to develop the habit of sucking their fingers or thumb. My reasoning was that it can lead to a child's natural gum and teeth layout being altered, which could then lead to a need for braces in future. The very few times prior to that moment that I had seen my daughter put her thumb in her mouth I had removed it.*

*However, my ex-husband decided to provoke me by encouraging her thumb sucking. I frustratingly looked on as he told her, "suck baby suck, let's annoy mummy". That was funny to him! I asked him to please stop doing that, and reiterated my point but his reply was, "It's my daughter and she could do what she wants, and if anybody touch her then I swear I will find them and kill them." I quickly rushed what I was doing and took over the childcare. Every time he cared for her I felt very anxious because I knew that his habit was to use it as an opportunity to irritate me.*

*Little things like that reinforced to me that my spouse got thrill and excitement out of making me annoyed. We were not on the same page; our goals, love and respect for each other were not aligned. He would do whatever he felt like, whenever he felt like it, no matter the short or long term consequences.*

# Consequences to Victims

Abuse in any form can lead to Injuries ranging from minor to severe. Top on the list of injuries are stress-related illnesses. Other consequences include long-term disabilities, unwanted pregnancies, abortion, lost work time, unemployment, poverty, children being taken into care, harm to children, parenting difficulties, depression, substance abuse, post-traumatic stress disorder and death.

Worldwide statistics indicate that on average a victim only begins to speak out about their life of being abused after three years. In my case that finding was spot-on. The following statistics shows a snippet of the scale of abuse that mainly women suffer at the hands of her partner. I have highlighted stats both in the United States of America and the United Kingdom. Let me also acknowledge that I know that domestic abuse is not just prevalent in those countries. Accessing any data on this topic is difficult and not accurate, because as mentioned many victims never report their abuser. Obtaining the data from other countries is even more difficult and in some instances nigh on impossible.

## Domestic Violence (DV) Statistics_____Data

## U.S.
Percent of women who have experienced DV_____25%
Estimated number of DV incidents per year_____960,000
Women Victims_____85%
On average, 3 females and 1 male are murdered by their partner each day
Women ages 20-24 are at the greatest risk
Number of children who witness DV annually_____6 Million +
Number of women who are stalked by an intimate partner annually_____503,485
Percent of DV crimes reported to police_____25%
Number of American women assaulted by men each year _____ 2,100,000
Percent of the victims of DV that are women_____95 %
Percent of all emergency room calls attributed to DV_____3.5 %

Percent of those that abuse their partner that also physically and/or sexually abuse their children_____65%
Number of women that die each day as a result of abuse_____4
Number of children that die each day as a result of abuse_____3
Percent of all women who sought care in hospital emergency rooms for violence related injuries_____37%
Number of women that are murdered by their husbands or boyfriends in this country every day_____2
Percent of violent crime experienced by men attributed to violence by an intimate partner _____2%

Source: U.S. Department of Justice, Bureau of Justice Statistics (Online)

Research Date: September 5th, 2014

http://www.statisticbrain.com/domestic-violence-abuse-stats/

# U.K. *(There are no reliable national data on the general incidence of domestic violence in the UK)\**
Percent of women who have experienced DV from age 16_____31%
Estimated number of DV incidents against women per year_____1.2million
Women Victims_____45%
Women under age 24 and those who have a long-term illness of disability are at the greatest risk
Number of children who witness DV annually_____750,000+
Percent of women who are stalked by an intimate partner annually_____9%
Percent of domestic crimes reported to police_____15%
Rate at which the police are called to respond to_____every 30 seconds
Number of times women ever experienced DV_____4+
Percent of all domestically abused women who had experienced violence more than 4 times_____89%
Percent of women in DV that result in physical injury or mental health issues___ 75%
Percent of the victims of domestic violence that are women_____61% - 90%
Percent of all emergency room calls attributed to_____10%
Percent of women that die as a result of abuse_____42%
Percent of female homicide victims killed by current or former partner_____ 36%+
Number of women at high risk of being murdered or seriously injured____100,000+
Number of children that die each week as a result of abuse and neglect_____1-3**
Percent of all women who sought care in hospital emergency rooms for violence related injuries_____37%

Number of women that are murdered by their husbands or boyfriends in
this country every week _____2
Percent of women victim of sexual abuse since the age of 16_____20%
Percent of DV that starts during pregnancy_____30%
Percent of incidents of DV, with children in the same or the next room____75%-90%
Percent of men who experience DV by an intimate partner from age 16_____18%
Percent of men who report having experienced DV abuse_____5%

Source: U.K.  www.WeWillSpeakOut.org

Contribution from: Office of National Statistics et al, Statistics on domestic
violence (online)

Report Date: May 2014

http://www.wewillspeakout.org/wp-content/uploads/2013/11/UK-
Statistics_May_2013.pdf

* Hester, Marianne (2008) Interpreting domestic violence data Paper
produced for the Home Affairs Select Committee, January 2008

**NSPCC (2014) Child killings in England and Wales, Explaining the statistics
March 2014

http://www.nspcc.org.uk/globalassets/documents/information-
service/factsheet-child-killings-england-wales-homicide-statistics.pdf

# Consequences to Children

Children who see others, especially their loved ones like mum, dad,
siblings etc, being victims of abuse are victims of abuse themselves.
This is so whether the abuser ever directly abuses them or not.
Furthermore, the younger the child the less able they are to walk away
from seeing or being in earshot of the incidents. The *NSPCC research on
child maltreatment (Radford, L et al. 2011)* showed that more than 34 per
cent of under-18s who had lived with domestic violence had themselves
been abused or neglected by a parent or guardian. It means then that
the abused parent is not just responsible for skilfully removing

themselves from that environment but they have the added pressure of being responsible for the protection or removal of the child from the abuser. If they don't, another link in the chain may be welded together and the cycle may repeat, with those children ultimately going through the same abuse later on in life.

Children who are forced to grow up in this type of environment where abuse is present can, without the proper support and training, end up abusing their own children. As adults they may get to a point where they do not see abuse as being wrong. They may totally not correct or discipline their offspring when they exhibit abusive behaviour, thereby possibly allowing them to abuse others from a young age. The children may begin to accept it as normal and even justify it being done. In support of this an article has been written by *Kantahyanee W. Murray et al (2012), Journal of family violence (Vol.27, Iss.6) The impact of intimate partner violence on mothers' parenting practices for urban, low-income adolescents pp 573-583.* In the study of whether intimate partner violence (IPV) affects mothers' ability in being a parent. They used a sample of 1,057 adolescent relationships in which the woman was the primary caregiver. The study found that women involved in abusive relationships are more likely to resort to physical punishment when disciplining their child and are less likely to get involved in their child's education.

An abuser will use anything in their power to control the victim, including destroying the victim's relationship with their children. When a mother feels too trapped to leave the relationship she begins to think of survival strategies for the safety of her children. These can include acting as a barrier between the abuser and the child if she feels like the child is in imminent danger. Another strategy is encouraging the child to stay away from the home as much as possible by them participating in things like extracurricular activities. Extreme approaches that are sometimes used for the child's protection are to send them to live with extended family, friends, to boarding school or to put them in the care of social services. Though this has the effect of moving the child to a safer environment, if the child does not fully understand why this is done or they end up unhappy at their new resident, it can have damaging effects on them. It is important that as much as is appropriate and possible, make the child aware of why it is in their best interest not to be at home with the abuser. Even above that the ideal thing to do in this scenario is for you to leave the abusive environment as well. You may have to live away from your child for a while as you rebuild financially. The message that you will be sending the child will be far greater than you remaining in abuse. Remember children are like sponges and they copy behaviour, even more than verbal instructions.

Children who see or experience sexual abuse from a close relative are severely affected. In a report by *Miranda A. H. Et al (2014) 'It's a lonely journey': a rapid evidence assessment on intrafamilial child sexual abuse pp 143*, the voice of child victims of this type of abuse is absent from research and prevalence is hard to estimate. They highlighted that in their opinion the UK child protection system is not child-centred so they can unknowingly end up subjecting victims of sexual abuse to secondary victimisation. In other words the number of sexual abuse cases that occur in the UK is greatly underestimated, particularly because the victims are not forthcoming with the information. Unless a child decides to open up to someone, and this may only happen if prompted, children are many times willing to keep this a secret. One of the reasons for a child holding on to the information may be threats made by the abuser. The abuser will at times threaten the victim by stating that it is within his power to kill one of their loved ones. Another reason is when the abuse starts while the child is very young and the abuser persuades them that what they are doing is not wrong.

The victim is sometimes told that their sexual violation is actually an expression of their love for each other.

Many mothers would like to believe that their relationship with their child is so open that the child shares everything with them. That is why many of them are shocked to find out from their child (in their later years as they feel more comfortable to open up) that they were being sexually abused, especially when it took place in their home. Sometimes the abuse could be going on for years and the mother wouldn't be aware of it. But this doesn't mean that she is to blame. The revelation of this type of abuse to a mother can be very hard hitting and may even affect her mental stability. Sexually abused children may begin to be given more freedom by the mother as she seeks to provide support and continue to lovingly function in her role as parent. Bear in mind that some of the parents are victims themselves. They may desperately now want to make the child feel happy, this sometimes causes them to compromise more in their role as parent. In an article by *Anna E. Jaffe et al (2012) Journal of child sexual abuse (Vol.21, No.6) Parenting in females exposed to intimate partner violence and childhood sexual abuse pp 684-700,* they examined the impact of child sexual abuse and intimate partner violence on parenting styles and the parenting self-efficacy of mothers. This was based on samples from a parenting intervention programme and a domestic violence shelter. In women from the parenting intervention programme, child sexual abuse was related to lower parenting self-efficacy and a more permissive parenting style. In women from the domestic violence shelter, child sexual abuse was related to current sexual coercion, indicating that a history of child sexual abuse should be taken into consideration in dealing with mothers in violent relationships.

Even though children are living through the effects of domestic abuse by law they are still expected to function normally during school time.

However, abuse does not remain indoors when the child leaves the home. In some countries like the UK and the USA and other advanced societies, when a child is identified as being in an unhealthy environment, help is normally offered to that child as soon as it is possible. At times different forms of abuse, be it what the child has seen or if they are personally violated, can affect the child's physical health. The topic was researched and made public by *Kate Ryan Kuhlman and Sandra A. Graham-Bermann (2012) Journal of family violence (Vol.27, Iss.6) Physical health in preschool children exposed to intimate partner violence pp 499-510.* The article considered the impact of exposure to domestic abuse on young children's physical health. The study was done on a sample of 102 pre-school children who had been exposed to domestic abuse. The findings concluded that children exhibiting more traumatic stress symptoms had fewer total health problems. It did note that gastrointestinal problems and asthma were related to poor psychological adjustment. The report also identifies girls as more likely to display health problems due to exposure to abuse than boys.

Another important aspect of children in abuse is that once the child is removed from the environment the abuser may become even more spiteful. It will be important that you disclose to the authorities about the full extent of your abuse and tendencies of the abuser so that a calculated decision will be made as to if the abuser should be given access to the child.

I removed myself and my daughter from the abusive environment when she was 1 year old. I knew the psychological effect that the situation would have on her had I stayed much longer. In the end, although I wanted freedom for myself I now had a greater reason to open my eyes to see and accept that my marriage and family dynamic was an unhealthy one.

If you are looking for a safe online community to share your thoughts, feelings and anxieties with then apply to join our secret Facebook group. Members are only added after we have approved them. We want to support you through your journey all the way to your freedom.

Go to: https://www.facebook.com/groups/MyChoiceMarriage

Key
Principle

We have to highlight the effects of abuse on everyone

in the situation. That includes the victim,

the abuser, the child and any

other dependants

CHAPTER 4

# IDENTIFYING THE SIGNS

# BEHIND AN ABUSIVE RELATIONSHIP

*"Choose to stop being the object of abuse, whether your abuser has inherent or learnt behaviour."*

☞ **Author** ☜

### Seeing the signs; don't ignore them

*My circle of friends was dwindling because of him. He made a habit of always telling me negative things that each of my friends had done to him. I later found out that most of the stories he told were either fabricated or exaggerated. At the same time there were women that I did not know who would telephone our house looking for him and they would address me as his sister.*

*Some of my friends would visit me occasionally but even while I spoke to them he would keep interrupting by calling me inside to ask trivial questions or to say something negative about them. I assumed that my friends didn't think much about these intrusions.*

*I remember an occasion when a relative came to visit and they asked me why he was calling me so many times. I held back my tears and acted as though everything was alright. When my friends had left and I was all alone, I started to speak to myself whilst engaging in some self-examination. 'Girl what are you doing?' I shouted.*

*I could not believe that I was the one living in so much fear and stress; believing that each day could be my last. Why was I sleeping on a bed with a man, who kept a military-style hunting knife under his pillow; who would regularly tell me about the atrocities that he could mete out on me and my family?*

*This was a defining moment for me. I came to realise that the starting point for moving forward was to take a step back, take a deep look at the situation and ask the simple question: 'how do I feel most of the time?'*

*No one deserves to be treated in a demeaning manner or to be controlled by another individual!*

*Abuse is wrong no matter what form it takes. People will continue doing what they do to you if you allow them to. When you see the first sign of this sort of treatment then you should forget your pride or trying to 'protect' your partner. Tell someone! One of my great mentors, Mr Les Brown says 'ask for help not because you are weak but because you want to remain strong and don't stop asking till you get it.'*

An abusive relationship is toxic to both individuals involved. While no type of abuse is excusable, there are times where individuals may say something emotionally abusive or send a hurtful text when they are in an argument with their spouse. These instances don't mean that the entire relationship is abusive; they just highlight where issues are present and signify that the couple should identify the abuse as what it really is, and work together to ensure that no more abuse takes place so that arguments and disagreements can be resolved in a constructive way. Other instances are where relationships centre on abusive behaviour and need to undergo drastic changes to ensure that both individuals are not only out of the relationship but stay safe and alive!

According to statistics for 2014, around 25% of teenage girls report that they experience repeated instances of verbal abuse in a relationship. Additionally, in both the US and UK, women between the ages of sixteen and twenty-four are at the highest percent for those who experience violence in intimate relationships. Another staggering statistic is that between seventy and eighty percent of homicide victims that are female have been murdered by their partner. The truth is that most abuse is never reported to the police yet it can end up in someone tragically dying either from suicide or homicide. Understanding the signs and symptoms of an abusive relationship is crucial to getting help early and preventing yourself, or someone you know, from becoming another tragic statistic.

# Signs of Abuse

- You are afraid of your partner or what he/she will do.
- You find yourself doing things you normally wouldn't do, or that you don't want to do, simply because your partner has insisted or bulled you into doing it.
- You feel horrible for spending time with others including family, friends, or even being at work. In other words unless he gives you permission, spending time away from your partner feels like a crime.
- You feel like you need to stay simply because your partner has said they will stop abusing you.
- You feel additional responsibility for whatever is happening in your partner's life. For example, if they're having problems, you feel as if it's your fault or that you're responsible for it.
- You have to tip toe around situations just so you don't upset or anger your partner and cause an argument.
- People tell you that they've not seen you that much anymore, or that you seem different recently.
- Your friends and family are picking up on your low self-esteem or down moods and commenting on it.
- You have a constant feeling of you not being able to do anything right in your relationship or to please your partner.
- You worry about being able to leave because you feel like you can't financially support yourself if you do.
- You feel compelled to stay with your partner because they've said that they are getting help for their 'anger' or counseling to help fix their problems.
- You find yourself only doing things for the other person and not yourself anymore. Your whole life revolves around theirs.

- You have a feeling of being trapped and not being able to get out of the situation or relationship.
- Your spouse or partner makes you feel poorly about yourself or disrespects you.
- You feel afraid to leave your partner because you believe something bad will happen.
- Your partner has previously been violent towards you or made violent threats towards you.
- Your partner blames their actions on you, especially when they get angry and break something or hurt someone.
- Your partner controls your finances or checks up on you. They have control of your life and know absolutely everything and you feel watched.
- Your partner is unpredictable and bad tempered.
- Your partner is very possessive and jealous.
- Your partner gets angry when you go out with friends or family and tells you not to anymore.

The list above is certainly not exhaustive but highlights the common signs that may be evident to you or others looking on. Now that you have read through this, you may be emotional or choose to stifle the feeling that comes up for you as reality sets in. I would suggest that once you are in a safe environment you should sit with that feeling, as you do continue to read through the chapters. You should also have a pen and paper ready to take notes, or you can scribble in your book if you feel safe to do so. Do not worry, I have outlined what you will need to do in order for you to make this violation of you a thing of your past.

# Identifying and Acknowledging that You're in an Abusive Relationship

The very first step to fixing the situation is to realize that you are not in a healthy relationship. People often skirt around the term "abusive" because it has many negative connotations to it, however when you finally add the label of abuse, you realize it for what it is: a toxic relationship. Abusive relationships are unhealthy for anyone involved, and children in that environment serve to complicate the situation and make it exponentially more dangerous. If you've checked at least one of the signs of an abusive relationship from the list above, then you need to stop and take a good hard look at your relationship.

Did you really picture yourself in the situation you are in now? Five years ago would you have thought you'd be in an abusive relationship? Or would you have much higher expectations of your life? The truth is that you do not deserve to be abused. It is not your fault, and there is a way out. I guarantee it. Now, you have to begin realizing that the person you're with isn't someone whom you truly love; he/she is an abuser, who may be putting up a facade. They're not that perfect image of a person you seem to think they can be some of the times; instead they're abusive, mean, and spiteful persons who don't truly love you. Think to yourself, if you truly loved someone, would you treat them the way you're being treated now? Don't make excuses for your abuser. Stop letting them get away with it. From now on, understand that the only way they treat you is how you let them treat you. That doesn't mean you have to try and retaliate, no you need to read the rest of this book and come up with a plan of action to get safely away from that environment.

Now that you're done making excuses and protecting your abuser, it's time for you to focus on the number one person in your life: yourself. If you have children, then you are even more important because you are the number one person in another's life as well. You need to be the strong, healthy, and happy role model that your children deserve. If your partner is not putting you at the top of their priority list, then you need to change the way you think relationships work. In fact, you should not only change your perception on your relationships but you need to also change your perception of yourself!

You see, saying 'I'm being abused' out loud or even mentally can be a scary process. No one wants to be abused and you sure as heck want it to stop. You want that picture perfect relationship you dreamed you would have when you got together with your partner, so stop settling for less. Identify how your partner is abusive to you and don't make excuses. Don't put any blame on yourself.

Does your partner ever hit you? Do they try and blame you and say that you've made them too angry and that's why they hit you? Don't fall for that excuse! They don't hit everyone who makes them angry; they just hit you because you're letting them get away with it! The first time they hit you is one time too many and you deserve far better!

Does your partner call you names like fat, ugly, slut, whore, or bitch? Verbal abuse is inexcusable and you deserve to be spoken to in a respectful way. Verbal abuse and emotional abuse can be just as painful as physical abuse; however they often go hand in hand. If the person you're with doesn't respect you or value you as a person, then they have no right to be involved in your life.

Does your partner control you or control your finances? Do they make up excuses and say that they don't trust you? Don't let them have excuses and don't let them control you. When you accept that behaviour, you're giving them the power to abuse you. Take it back and don't stand for being controlled. No one should have the power to tell you what you can and cannot do.

Now that you've identified you're in an abusive relationship, you've already taken the first step. Now the real work begins!

When I first identified that I was in an abusive relationship I got filled with mixed emotions. As a Christian I was praying to God that the relationship would change before anyone realised what I was putting up with. I regretted ever having the first conversation that I had with my husband. I wished he had never been born. I wished he would stop making threats and hurry up and kill me but that he wouldn't get away with it. I wished I had the physical evidence at the time to show others the things he was doing when they were not looking. The conversations in my head kept changing every 5 minutes. Then, there were the lies he would tell me in order for me to have sex with him. When the lies didn't work he resorted to using bible quotes to justify that it was my duty. The sad thing is that as a victim of abuse we get comfortable sitting in the mess; it begins to feel warm and somewhat cosy. The problem is that mess doesn't only stink, it also is destroying. Just like you shouldn't leave faeces on the inside, when it comes out you should not leave it hanging around you. As a mum when I discover that my baby has done a number two, I remove it from her skin as soon as is possible. If you have never witnessed the consequences of leaving a baby with soiled diaper just Google it.

What am I saying? Keeping the fact that you are being abused all to yourself or remaining in the relationship while you wait for him to change are both equally detrimental to you. According to the *World Health Organisation (2000), in their factsheet No 239* 'abused women are more likely to suffer from depression, anxiety, psychosomatic systems, eating problems and sexual dysfunction. Violence may also affect their reproductive health.' You cannot stay in an abusive relationship and function at your highest level of self. To you, you may be functioning at your peak. You may believe that all your spouse does or says is like water off your back. The reality is that consciously and unconsciously all that he does, he says and implies is getting deep into your inner being and affecting who you really are. You need to break free and it all starts with identifying the type of relationship you are in. Is it a healthy relationship? If the answer is no, then the next step is to admit it; first to yourself then to others. As you read on in this book you will be offered guidance on who you should confide in about your situation.

I would like to invite you to join us as we launch a campaign to help stop women and men from entering the cycle of abuse.

## The 'No Strikes' Campaign

"No Strikes™" is a worldwide movement of domestic abuse survivors and supporters, who are coming together against spousal abuse. Our slogan is "One strike and I'll Shout, Two strikes and I'm Out™". We want to empower women and men not to put up with any form of abuse. We want people to know that they can stop this heinous pattern of behaviour as soon as it rears its head by not just speaking out but by following through. Don't put up with disrespect and abuse under any circumstance. You deserve respect. Go to this link to share your story http://www.mychoicemarriage.com/no-strikes.

Key
Principle

We should examine why abusers do what they do;

as long as we emphasise that nothing

justifies their actions.

CHAPTER 5

# THE FOUNDATIONS OF ABUSE

*"One method that your abuser uses to control you is by allowing you the occasional indulgence."*

☞ **Author** ☜

### Manipulation is a puppet string

*It had been ten days that he hadn't come home. Late that night I decided to call his mother to ask her if she knew where he was. I was also going to tell her that I had not seen him for almost two weeks.*

*My mother in law was so surprised to hear from me. She said that she too had no idea where her son was. She then asked me why I was saying such bad things about them and that she knew I didn't come around to see her and the rest of his family because I thought I was better than them.*

*"What? That is a lie from the pit of hell!" I told her in response to the shocking allegations. I then told her the things that I had heard from her son. The things she had said about me and my family was the reason why her son did not come around much.*

*That is when it dawned on me; we were both being lied to. Actually manipulated is the correct word. The tactic was clearly communicated: my mother in law and I were to hate each other so that he could be free to do as he pleases because both our families were not in a position to communicate with one another. As a result of this, there would be no one he would be accountable to. I also began to realise the pattern of him doing to same thing over and over again. One by one he had been destroying my relationship with my friends.*

*As I am writing this I can now vividly remember him trying it with every member of my extended family that he knew. The only reason why those attempts did not work was because of my love and forgiving nature towards those close to me. For the other relationships that were affected I want to publicly apologise. My ex husband's fabrications were in many cases both very elaborate and convincing. I just need to state here that if I never meet some of you again in person, I absolutely hold no malice against you.*

*The lesson here is that you should never hold back, instead you should communicate. Feel free to ask questions and engage in open dialogue. The secret is to keep on talking. When you talk you give the abuser minimal ground for spreading the seeds of discord. In short, information is power and it leaves everything in the open for everyone to see.*

On average, there are over twelve million reported people who are victims of physical violence each year. Additionally, around twenty-nine percent of women in the United States have reported being raped, physically abused, and/or stalked by a partner. This is according to the Bureau of Justice statistic. It means that with such staggeringly high statistics you have likely seen and met many victims of abuse in your lifetime and subsequently abusers as well. So who are abusers and their victims? Why do people abuse in the first place and why do their victims allow the abuse to continue?

## Understanding Abusers

The answer to why someone becomes an abuser is never simple. Usually there are many contributing factors and understanding the reasoning behind abuser's actions is difficult. One main reason that many individuals become abusers is because they witnessed or were victims of abuse themselves. Perpetuating the cycle of abuse is common because the behaviours that children learn in their younger years are often repeated when they're adults.

While listing all of the potential reasons behind an abuser's actions is not possible for this book, you can begin to understand some of the main reasons why most people abuse. Keeping in mind that approximately ninety-one out of a hundred domestic abusers will be men; consider these following causes and potential motives for an abuser's actions below:

## Nature

The debate between whether its nature or nurture plays a bigger part in an individual's life is one of the driving forces behind many psychological and theoretical debates. When considering abusers and the statistics that have been accrued over years of studying families, it has been discovered that nurture is a larger contributing factor for abusive tendencies (both for those who allow themselves to be victims, and also for those who become abusers themselves) however nature still plays a role.

Some individuals are born with a higher affiliation for physical violence, control, anxiety, and mental problems. In the case of abusers, these natural qualities and tendencies significantly increase the risk of a person becoming abusive but don't guarantee it. There are vast numbers of individuals with mental health issues, anxiety and control problems, and also affinities for violence that do not become abusive to their partners.

## Mental Health Problems

There are millions of individuals in the world who are diagnosed with a mental health condition. Some mild conditions, such as mild anxiety or sporadic depression can be managed successfully with a bit of therapy. Other conditions, such as schizophrenia, autism, Alzheimer's, and oneirophrenia can cause individuals to be far more likely to abuse their partners as a side effect of their mental condition. Consider the following mental health issues and if any of them is a factor in your home:

- Personality disorders – individuals with personality disorders such as schizoid personality disorder, schizophrenia, borderline personality disorder and others can exhibit violent tendencies towards their partners and other people. These personality disorders and mental conditions are generally treated with a combination of medications and therapy. There are many patients who refuse treatment or have not been properly diagnosed by professionals.

These individuals will likely continue to display their erratic and potentially aggressive and violent behaviour.

- Anxiety – A marked trait of individuals with high anxiety is that they attempt to seize control of situations to help calm their fears. This need for control, and the subsequent anxiety that is felt when they aren't in control, can be a contributing factor towards behaviour of abusers. When someone feels the constant need to be in control they may become financially or emotionally abusive towards their partners.

In many relationships, an individual with high anxiety may feel that their partner will leave them for someone else, or that they will cheat on them with previous partners. To help keep their feelings of anxiety under control, the abuser will emotionally and verbally abuse their partners to prevent them from going out and possibly doing what it is they fear. This constant need for control can lead to relationships where a single individual has all of the power and control, and the other is merely a victim.

- Depression – individuals who are depressed often don't act out violently. However, they may attempt to self-medicate through alcohol and substance abuse. When this occurs, depressed individuals may lash out physically or verbally towards their partners and anyone else around them. Avoiding self-medication is crucial to ensuring that the individual gets the correct help for their problems.

- Another reason why depression can be a contributing factor towards an abuser's actions and continued abuse is a lower self-esteem and self-worth. If an abuser doesn't believe they're worthy, or that they're a good person or has low self-esteem for another reason, they may seek to hold onto their partner by abusing them. The need to help soothe the fears and symptoms of depression is common but for individuals who are prone to exhibiting abusive tendencies, depression only fuels their actions.

# Nurture

Out of all the potential causes or motivations behind an abuser's actions, the way a person is brought up (their family life, culture, religion, schooling, friends, etc.) plays the most vital role. The problem is that when children are brought up in an abusive household, or in a bad neighbourhood, then they are statistically higher to become abusive, violent, and even turn to actions that lead them to criminal offenses.

## Perpetuation of the Cycle

The problem with children growing up in a household where one or both of the parents are abusive (financially, emotionally, verbally, physically, sexually), they are led to believe that those actions are normal and that what they are seeing is a healthy relationship between two adults. Unfortunately, as you may know, when abuse occurs in relationships then it is highly toxic to both individuals, even if it is not physical. Consider these horrific statistics below that were obtained from the RAINN.org website (Rape, Abuse & Incest National Network).

Extensive studies done on families with domestic violence and abuse. These statistics were discovered:

- When boys were found from families of domestic violence they themselves were three times more likely to then abuse their partners as adults.
- Boys from abusive households and families are found to have a seventy-four percent greater chance of then committing crimes against others as teenagers and adults.

- Boys from abusive households and families were found to have a much higher chance of committing sexual assault or rape against another individual when they were adult. The statistics found that the chance of this happening was about twenty-five times more likely than a boy from a household where abuse was not present.
- Male adults from the studies who grew up in an abusive household were found to be a thousand times more likely to abuse their own children.
- When women grow up in abusive households, they are found to statistically be 6.51 times more likely to be sexually abused, especially if the father is physically abusive towards the mother.
- The last vital statistic that was found is that children (both girls and boys) who are from households where abuse took place are found to be fifty percent more likely to turn towards substance abuse including drugs and alcohol.

## Substance Abuse

Many individuals who are abusive also drink alcohol or take drugs. The substance abuse may be the root cause for an individual to be abusive towards their partner, or it may only enhance the frequency and severity of the abuse. Whatever the case, the correlation between drugs and alcohol along with abuse in relationships is a positive one.

A huge problem with abusers is that alcohol slows down their cognitive processes, makes it difficult to reason, and distorts situations. Because of all the symptoms and sensations that alcohol causes, it can easily enhance the aggressive nature of certain individuals. There are many people who are only abusive when drinking, and who don't remember abusing their partner at all. Regrettably, there are many more individuals who abuse their partners on a regular basis and only use alcohol to dull their emotional pain while ignoring their knowledge of how they act while inebriated. The number of reported instances of physical abuse that occurs when individuals have drunk alcohol is far greater than those that occur without anyone drinking alcohol.

# The Narcissist

Some abusers actually have low self-esteem which they camouflage by overasserting their authority and exaggerating their worth and achievements. They are normally very attention seeking; especially from the rich and famous. They operate with an attitude of entitlement which helps them to feel powerful and unique. The action of the narcissist is self-serving in nature, whether it is to their spouse, family members or co-worker. They enjoy manipulating and controlling vulnerable people and take pleasure in squashing their sometimes unsuspecting victim's self-confidence. A narcissist has the 'Jekyll and Hyde' persona, in public they charm – in private they harm their victim. They can become even more evil if their private personality is revealed because they have an enlarged ego that continually needs to be stroked.

According to online reports about 1.06% of individuals are clinically narcissistic and more have characteristics of personality disorder.

To this day I keep asking myself the question, what would make a 21 year old man ask the 19 year old to marry her, saying it is God ordained, and then start abusing her from the time they are on honeymoon? I may never know the answer. What is obvious is that something in his past, be it inherent on learnt behaviour, made him do it comfortably and unrepentant about his actions.

As I have stated in previous chapters, you have to keep reminding yourself that putting up with damaging behaviour from someone, especially when it is directed at you or your loved ones does not serve anyone. Even when you have to face the reality that their behaviour is inherent to them, you do not have to remain the object of their terror. In my opinion, the best thing that you can do for that person is to love them from afar. Having someone disrespect you as a person and belittle you - be it in private or public - is causing you untold harm. Again, you may not even realise the level of negative impact it is having on you as a person, but I can assure you that it is. It took me years to come to terms with the degree of damage that had taken place within me. Although some of the effects were evident from the beginning, I thought that because I had left the environment I was free. The fact is that I was physically free from harm's way, but mentally and as I have been discovering health wise, I am still healing and working through some of the injuries. Limit the negative, hurtful effects of abuse by making the decision to remove yourself safely from what I have now termed

## 'Intimate Slavery'.

'Intimate Slavery' is used to describe that you are being or were controlled by your spouse in your intimate relationship, instead of being loved. The length of your imprisonment is dependent on the length of time that you remain silent. The longer you stay quiet, the tighter the grip on your mind becomes. Your slave master' typically has a number of aims: to stop you from thinking independently; to quash your desire to live your life freely and ultimately to groom you into believing that your slavery doesn't in fact exist.

The particular type of abuse used is not the primary issue, rather, it is the fact that your freedom to live independently, fearlessly or happily has been taken from you at some point in time. Another important factor of 'Intimate Slavery' is the psychological effect that it has on you exponentially outlasts the time you remove your physical self from the situation.

An 'Intimate [slave] Master' is someone that enslaves and silences you in your relationship with them. They seek to control all aspects of your life but with one or a combination of the following criterion:

- Without making their controlling behaviour public knowledge
- Convincing others that you deserve to be controlled
- Convincing others that you can't think independently

You must free yourself from this slavery by opening up about its existence in your life, whether its existence is in the past or present. Individuals who decide not to share with authorities, or with others that can help them heal, remain under the grip of the 'Intimate Master'.

Key
Principle

In abusive situations there are two things happening

simultaneously; the abuser is controlling you but

you are also allowing the abuser to control you.

In other words the abuser gives and the

victim accepts what is being given

CHAPTER 6

# HOW ABUSERS CONTINUE TO

# CONTROL AND ABUSE THEIR VICTIMS

*"Which is worse a black eye or a mental breakdown*
*caused by abuse? You answer..."*

 **Author**

**A silly reason to stay in abuse - don't do the same!**

*That day I was at my childhood home standing around the dining room table.*
*The Caribbean sun was hot but so was the situation inside as my husband*
*continued sharing more lies about me to my mum. One of the lies was that he*
*doesn't eat because I do not cook. This went on and on and so I got fed up.*

*"Mummy he hits me!" I told my mother in his presence. He tried to change the topic as if what I said didn't matter and he called my mother by his nickname for her, "Ms Claudie."*

*" Do not Ms Claudie me, you do what to my daughter?!"*

*My mother's reaction made me nervous and I was the one changing the topic now since I was afraid that she would get sick or even do something that she will regret.*

*I didn't speak about the issue for the next three years.*

*What's the lesson in all this? Well the truth of the matter is that you do not know what the reaction will be when you open up. If you anticipate that it will be a negative reaction that will make you shut down then find someone else to open up to if necessary.*

*Why do I say so? Well in my situation the abuse didn't stop. It only aggravated it and things continued to get worse. I was the one who encouraged the intimate slavery to persist, by my silence.*

*As the cycle continued I pretended that all was well; I wondered why others would take it. At that time I still didn't realise I was one of the ones taking it. I held on to the lies that he told me. Of all the conversations he had with me 95% was manipulation, coercion, blame, shame, threats, physical jabs and a lot more. For a while I convinced myself that I could help him change but the truth is I couldn't.*

# Popular Methods to Keep Control over Victims

Despite there being many reasons behind why people abuse, there is absolutely no valid excuse for it to happen even once. The first time that a person is abused, they should seek immediate help in preventing it from happening ever again, yet this rarely happens. All too often you hear of people who are in abusive relationships for years, only getting out when the situation becomes too physically unbearable. Additionally, the number of homicides reported yearly is saddening, especially when one takes a chance to look and realizes that a high percentage of homicides that are between spouses have had previous incidents of reported abuse. So why are abusers allowed to continue their horrendous acts? It's likely because they've not only perfected the process of manipulating and controlling their victims but it is also because a relationship hardly ever starts out abusive.

If you think back to the beginning of the relationships you've been in, you've likely had great times with your partners. The beginning of most relationships is often the best time – you hardly ever argue, you get along well, you don't live together, there is nothing major shared (house, bills, bank account, etc.). Many times because you're still getting to know the person, you are willing to ignore any seemingly insignificant negative/violating displays of communication or behaviour towards you. It is only after a while that most abusers begin revealing the extent of their dark and controlling side – the side of their personality that doesn't love their partner, instead it wants to dominate, hurt, and control. As the relationship progresses and people get more and more invested both with money and time, the more an abuser will reveal the controlling and domineering aspects of their personality.

In an attempt to charm you, information that an abuser reveals to you at the start of your relationship may actually only be what they think you want to hear. They fill your mind with false hopes, fabricated fantasy and any other information that will grab your attention. This doesn't mean that they only make themselves look good. Actually another popular tactic is to present themselves as victims, people misunderstood, someone respected by many but hated by others.

Additionally, abusers perfect a process and set method that works on their victims. They not only isolate their victims and intimidate them but they use their power to dominate their partner and enable the abuse to continue.

- Isolation – this is a key component to the success of an abuser. Most of the time, if the victim has a support group of friends and family around them, then the abuse will not go unnoticed. Family members and friends normally want the best for victims and will hopefully not encourage them to stay with an individual who harms them or hurts them purposefully. It is because of this that abusers work so hard to isolate their victim.

  One way that isolation occurs is by turning the victim on the family themselves. Causing problems between the victim and their family or friends ensures that the only support the victim has is the abuser.

  Another way an abuser is able to isolate their victim is by forcing the victim to not keep contact with the outside world. That includes extended family and friends, religious and other social groups etc. This is done by constantly making the victim feel guilty about spending time away from the abuser, or by intimidating the victim into not seeing their friends/family. Understanding that a healthy relationship can allow both your family/friends and your partner to be in your life is key to ensuring that you are never isolated and vulnerable to an abuser!

- Coercion – throughout an abusive relationship a victim is often led to believe things will change through coercion. An abuser will constantly promise "I'll never hit you again", or "I'm getting help soon!" An abuser will come up with a million excuses as a way to coerce the victim into staying in the relationship and not leave!

- Threats/Intimidating – during the more intensive stages of an abusive relationship, an abuser will often begin using threats and intimidation as a way to control their victim. This is usually done after they have isolated the victim from their family and friends, however it can easily happen in the beginning as well. Threats can be ones of physical harm if the victim does not do as the abuser demands, or it can be ones such as:

  o " I'll kick you out and you'll be homeless if you don't do as I say!"
  o "I'll get you fired from work if you don't do as I say!"
  o "I'll take the children from you and they'll hate you if you leave me!"

Unfortunately the more power and control a victim gives their abuser, the more an abuser has to threaten them with! An abuser will always use every tool in their arsenal to their advantage – especially if they feel that the victim may leave them or seek outside help!

- Children – another unfortunate yet vital weapon that abusers use to control their victims are children. Children frequently become pawns and suffer greatly when their parents are in abusive relationships. Some ways children can be used to control victims are as follows:

  o "I'll never let you see the children again if you don't do what I want you to"
  o "I'll tell the kids how horrible you are and they'll hate you"
  o "No man/woman will want to be with you because you've got children. I'm the best you can get"

    o    "I'll kick you out of the house and take you to court so I get full guardianship of the children"

When abusers and their victims have children, the situation becomes far more complicated and can often shift in the abuser's favour. Many people will choose to stay in abusive relationships when children are involved simply because they want to ensure their kids have "two parents in their lives", a "nice house to live in", "a good school to go to", and many more things. It is important to know that NO child will benefit if their parents are in an unhealthy and abusive relationship. In fact, as you saw from the staggering statistics earlier, the damage done to children when the parents are abusers/abusive is lifelong and can cause them to not only turn towards drugs and alcohol but also become abusers/victims themselves!

- Denial – the denial that there is a problem, that abuse took place, or that the abuse was intentional is another key tool in an abusers method to ensure that they can continue abusing their victims. The victim may feel as if they're going mad, as if they're imagining things, or as if no one will believe them in this case – ensuring that they don't leave the relationship. Additionally, denial often happens in the beginning when abuse first surfaces in a relationship. As it is denied, the abuser realizes they are allowed to get away with more and they learn to continue abusing their victims and denying it further.

- Minimization – hand in hand with denial is minimization. An abuser will say things such as "I didn't really punch you; I just hit you lightly with my hand when you frustrated me!" The minimization of their actions also encourages the victim to minimize it in their own minds, making it easier to accept and easier to stay in an abusive relationship. Minimization is an incredibly effective tool of manipulation that abusers use constantly both to authorities, victims, and bystanders.

- Shifting Blame – putting the blame on the victim is a crucial tool of manipulation that serves two purposes for the abuser. First it allows them to keep abusing their victims because their victims don't think the abuser actually did anything wrong. Secondly, a victim actually loses self-confidence and esteem because they feel as if they're punished for a reason, as if they need to be abused. Long term victims of abuse will often be heard saying "Oh, well if I didn't do that he wouldn't have gotten so mad and hit me". They actually believe that the abuse is their fault, when it NEVER is. The abuse is never the fault of the victim. Another way the abuser shifts the blame is by accusing the victim of doing all the things that they have done or are still doing. The victim may begin to believe that something in their action is sending out that signal, which can cause them to adopt an even more unduly subdued attitude. If you're involved in an abusive relationship you need to tell yourself that there is absolutely no reason why someone should emotionally, physically, or verbally abuse you even in the slightest! You must try your best not to allow their accusations to affect your personality.

- Degrading/Emotional Abuse – lastly, a tool that allows abusers to continuously control and harm their victims is degrading them and emotional abuse. Abusers will often not only isolate their victims but make them feel as if they're not desired, loved, or wanted by anyone else but the abuser. This allows the victim to become completely dependent on the abuser, makes them feel as if they don't deserve anyone else, and allows the abuser to convince the victim that the abuse is acceptable.

## Why People Allow Themselves to be Abused?

Abusers do everything they can to convince their victims to stay. From coercion, intimidation, degradation, and even minimization, there are a plethora of ways that abusers use to manipulate and control their victims. Unfortunately, the victims themselves often adopt a mentality that allows them to accept the abuse and continue with the relationship. There is likely a wide variety of reasons why people stay past the first instance of abuse, however some of the main ones that victims have reported are:

• Fear of being alone

Humans in general are incredibly social animals. We desire the company of others, and having a partner to share life with is something that almost everyone wants. Families, husbands, wives, and lovers all are something that is not only desired but normal in our society. So when someone is in a relationship, the prospect of being without that life partner is a daunting one.

Take, for instance, a middle aged woman who has been married to her husband for ten years now. He's abused her several times over the course of her marriage but she's never left him not only because she's got kids but because they're married. They've been married many years, she's planned her life with this man and all of their friends are married as well. The idea of being a single mother in her middle ages of life is something that scares her and she never even thinks of divorce because of it!

Regrettably when someone is abusive to their partner, they don't truly love them. There are certain things that you don't do to the person you love, and one of them is hurt them intentionally – especially physically.

A person is never alone because there are always friends and family, no matter how distant they may be due to isolation. Staying with a person purely for the sake of not being alone means that a situation will never get better; more time is simply wasted being unhappy and missing out on potential happiness!

- Too much time invested

The amount of time a person has invested into a relationship also plays a massive role in their decision to stay or leave at the first sign of abuse. While most people would take an instance of abuse and immediately leave knowing that it wasn't acceptable, others may see throwing years 'down the drain' rather than see the unacceptable behaviour in that relationship. When people become married, have children, and have been together for many years, they are more likely to accept forms of abuse and not leave the relationship as opposed to when abuse occurs within the first year of the relationship.

- Think that they can change the other person

Often women feel the need to be a nurturing partner and 'help' others. Unfortunately it is this key trait that abusers feed on and use against the victim. Abusers who have alcohol or drug problems rely heavily and become dependent on their victims. This is a sure way for the abuse to continue through coercion and constant reassurance to their victim that things will get better and that they can change.

While everyone has problems and everyone has some sort of emotional baggage that they bring into a relationship, none should be so severe that they need to rely heavily on their partner. This creates an imbalance of power. Moreover, you can never put in a hundred percent into a relationship when you still need to fix yourself, so allowing yourself to accept a partner with problems only opens up the door to an abusive relationship! You cannot fix another person – they can only fix themselves. Helping others is a great thing. However, you need to ensure that the number one person in your life (yourself) is taken care of first!

- Think that abuse is normal

The idea that abuse is normal is a foreign concept to most people, especially when they are observing other relationships and identifying the abuse that takes place. Sadly, when people are raised in abusive households, the idea that adults treat each other in abusive ways is something that becomes normal. Furthermore, if they are abused themselves, the concept of being aggressive and abusive towards other individuals is instilled into them and they are more likely to become abusive not only to their partners when they are adults but also to their children as well.

Another way that abuse can seem normal is if a person grows up in an area where aggression, abuse, and violence are commonplace. The friends that a person surrounds themselves with, especially in their vital teenage years, helps dramatically shape their ideas and beliefs which is why a great neighbourhood is crucial to ensuring the health and safety of children throughout their life.

- Don't seek help

Seeking help either through proper authorities (police, advocate groups, etc), or through friends and family is something that can help abuse be stopped in its tracks the very instance it occurs. Unfortunately abusers realize that outside interference can immediately sever their control and hold on their victims. This is why they work so hard to isolate their victims. Seeking help is essential – either through self-help books, support groups, online forums, chat lines, family members, and especially from the authorities!

There is always someone there to help you, no matter how alone or upset you may feel at the time. You are never alone and there is always a way out if you are strong enough to ask for the help. An abusers worst nightmare is when their victim breaks out of their isolating grip!

- Children

As mentioned before, an abuser will use children in myriad ways to help coerce and convince their victims to stay. It is sad to say but a victim will also create excuses and reasons to stay themselves, allowing the relationship and subsequent abuse to continue.

Some excuses that victims use when children are involved are:

"I can't financially support myself and my kids if I leave"

"I don't want my children growing up without both parents there"

"He's a great dad to the kids – he's never hurt them once and never will!"

"The kids don't see the abuse so they're not affected by it".

The truth is that the children are affected by it, even if the abuse isn't happening right in front of them, even when they are in the house or out of the house at the time. Having a parent that is abused and stayed in abusive relationships simply teaches the children that it is acceptable and that's how adults behave in relationships. Moreover, there is no telling whether or not an abuser will switch from becoming violent to their partner to also becoming violent towards children as well. Just because a child is young, when they become teenagers there is always the high risk they will also become abused!

- Embarrassed

Saying "I've been abused" may be embarrassing for victims to say, especially when the victims are well known and well respected. No one likes to admit that they are a victim because it implies a weakness of sort. Fortunately this is never true and the fact that they are the victims of abuse does not make them less in any way!

- Culture/religion

Culture and religion are two massive reasons why victims stay in abusive relationships. There are some cultures where divorce is completely seen or treated as illegal, while in others the man has all of the power and is actually allowed to abuse their partners. To judge and say that an entire culture, belief, or religion is 'wrong' because of its views on spousal relationships or gender roles is something that this book doesn't attempt to do. However, it is vital to understand that every person is important. Every person, man or woman, deserves to be safe, happy, and healthy. If there is something impeding that, such as an abusive spouse or a dominating husband, then that is wrong. No one deserves to be physically or emotionally abused by another person!

- Disability/illness

There are many cases where a person may be disabled or ill and where they become dependent on their partner. When one person becomes more dependent on another, they do so with the belief that their partner will treat the added power and responsibility with respect and do what is in the best interest of the relationship. All too often, however, there are reports where people with disabilities are abused and those who have illnesses are neglected. Those who are disabled or ill will often justify the abusive behaviours because of lower self-esteem, thinking that no one else will be with them because of their physical or mental problem.

No matter what the abuser has gone through before the relationship, or what reasons a victim uses to justify the actions of their abusive partner, there is no excuse for abuse to ever take place. Remember that a relationship needs to have both partners respected for it to be healthy and productive. Someone who abuses (financially, emotionally, verbally, or physically), does not truly respect and love their partner. Making excuses for an abuser only allows a situation to get worse!

*While I remained in the abusive relationship I used a combination of excuses as to why I should stick it out. My main reason was religious duties. It was almost ignoring the parts of the bible that speaks about us being in good health, about how a husband is supposed to love and cherish his wife and how God wants us to be abundantly happy. From the time I got on honeymoon and my ex refused to take me to the beach, because as he put it 'his grandmother said that we must always go on the beach with a crowd,' I should have taken that as an indicator of how he wanted to change who I was to his own end. Now bear in mind that when we met I was still at secondary school. I was an avid volleyball player who played for my school's team. Many evenings I would go down to the beach, sometimes on my own just to practice so that I could improve my skills. While there, friendly people will normally come over and have a go playing with me. My point is that he met me going to the beach with my mother's permission. He sometimes came down and saw me there. So to now decide that what I normally do, not to mention one of the main reasons why couples go on tropical holiday and honeymoon was not allowed, well I was in shock.*

*After four days of asking on my own and now in tears, I got some elderly family friends to also speak to him. He finally agreed to take me late one evening. As soon as we got there, he spotted a group of men playing beach football and he decided that he would go join in. At 6pm the Caribbean Sea water felt too cold and uninviting that day. The sun had gone down and the tropical breeze felt chilly before I had even sampled the water. I dipped my toe at the shore line and imagined how much more inviting it must have been earlier that day. I then decided to just sit and wait for him to finish his kick-about. Just then a Rastafarian walked by. I was startled as he took my left hand quickly kissed it and called me Nubian princess. Before I had the chance to react he went on his way with a smile on his face. My first thought was 'what just happened?' Followed by 'did my husband see what just transpired?' well' I should have left it at that and not bring up the topic unless he did.*

*He finished his game all bubbly and excited and we walked away from the sea side on our way back to where we were staying. After we had walked a few kilometres I began to relay to him my encounter with the Rasta man. I anticipated a reaction like 'why would he think it's ok to just kiss the hand of a random woman without her permission?' Well I was far from accurate in my assumption. In a quick rambling and colloquial manner he said, "He did what? Who is that man dread? He don't want me to kill him?" As the shock of his response reached my brain I watched him as he lifted up one leg of his trousers by the seam, reached into his sock and pulled out his military-style hunting and combat knife. Before I could finish asking, "What are you doing?" He started briskly walking back toward to beach, then after a few steps he began to run. Well I was in a daze; shock, frantic and shouting for him to stop and not get himself in trouble. In an attempt to stop him I began to run after him and brought on the water works. He finally relented when I said the guy has long gone by now. Puffing and panting he stopped running, turned around and slowly walked toward me letting me know how he will kill anyone who tried to hurt me.*

That whole situation was confusing to me at the time. I tried to make sense of it all. That got my marriage of to an interesting start but within a few days the words he used had moved from what he could do to others to what he could do to me. It also became normal for us to take a taxi together, him drop me off at my mother's house as he continued on his journey to go out to cinema or out with friends.

I look back now and wonder why I put up so long. I had to forgive myself for remaining in that situation all those days past my honeymoon. I thought about all the family, friends, loved ones, well wishers, critics, naysayers etc who are watching on at the relationship. I tried desperately to make the broken, unhealthy union work. There is a saying 'if it ain't broke don't fix it'. On the other hand 'if it was never a perfect pair stop pretending that it ever was.' In total I remained nine years in that relationship, six of it as a frustrated woman more than a wife, it was time for me to give myself the marching papers. I had passed the use by date; it was time to formulate a plan, it was Time To Go!

There are many books that go in depth about abusers; how and why they do what they do. For further study into their behaviour and characteristics I highly recommend that you have a look at a number of handpicked resources on the topic. Choose the ones that will give you the answers that you are looking for.

Go to http://www.relationship121.com/abuse for the list.

Key
Principle

It is time that we stop judging abuse by bruises.

All abused victims are in a prison, they are

undeservingly being controlled and

manipulated by a selfish,

conniving human being

CHAPTER 7

# DECIDING WISELY

# TO LEAVE YOUR ABUSIVE SPOUSE

*"To decide simply means that you have chosen*
*De [the] side you want to be on."*

☞ **Author** ☜

**When you know in your heart it's Time To Go!**

*Then fear took over. I was afraid of leaving but I was also afraid of staying. The*
*threats were becoming too much. He was leaving home and staying away for*

weeks at a time even more frequently. Whenever he came back it was clear that I had no authority to ask him where he'd been.

The thing was, I was never sure where he was going and what he did while he was away. This led to worry flooding my thoughts. The main worry was about my health - he could be introducing STDs into our marriage. I was forced to come up with every excuse I could find in order for us to use protection whenever he wanted intercourse. The most inventive of all being that I did not want to get pregnant - it worked.

Once I was offered lots of condoms by my local health centre which I was reluctant to take but finally I did take them. When I got home I put them in a drawer and did not pay a lot of attention to them apart from telling him that one of us should be using them.

One day I went to the drawer and the condoms were gone. When I asked him about them, he gave an excuse of his friends coming by and asking for them. The condoms being taken away, the abuse, being worried about death every single day and losing my personality in the whole process was a combination that I could only describe as being too much. Still to those who did not suspect anything, I pretended that "all was well in paradise".

Here the lesson was to wake up and smell the coffee. This was no way for anyone to live. It was up to me to open my eyes to all the signs of truth that was around me. The battle between the tangible and intangible was set. What will you choose? Will you choose the man and his money (no matter how unhappy you are) or will you choose your confidence, self-esteem and energy?

You should open your mind, imagine and believe in what is possible for you when you leave this Intimate Slavery.

Once you've deduced that you're in a toxic and abusive relationship, the next step is to leave as safely and quickly as possible. You need to tell yourself these four important truths on a regular basis:

- Your abuser does not truly love you, no matter what he/she says.
- You are not responsible for your abuser's life or actions; you are responsible for you alone!
- He controls you not because you need him but rather he is so dependent on you and he can't see the relationship ending at all.
- This is absolutely not a healthy relationship or way to live.

Pushing out any thoughts of 'helping' your abuser because they claim to love you and they claim that they just need time and patience to change is not going to fix the situation at all. Abusers only change when they are forced to change – when you leave them for good and they are faced with the reality of what they've done. Additionally, when you stay in an abusive relationship you are completely enabling your abuser – allowing them to continue with their behaviours. You're letting yourself and your children, if you have any, be put in constant danger so it's time to make a change and leave.

# Making The Decision

As we stated earlier, there are varying degrees of abuse that can occur in a relationship. While absolutely any form of abuse is completely unacceptable, it is key to understand that people often say things in the heat of an argument that they wouldn't normally say. So should you leave a relationship just because some verbally abusive things were said in anger during a heated argument? Or should you wait until things get physical? Is there some defined line that can be drawn at some point, or how do you know when to leave a relationship when things become 'too abusive'.

For a start, let's take a look at two very different examples of abuse and consider appropriate responses to them.

**Example One** – A husband and wife are arguing over whether or not to ask the wife's mother for a small loan. The husband was recently let go at a previous job and, while he is currently employed, he doesn't get a pay check for some time yet and there are bills to be paid. The wife insists to ask the mother, while the husband doesn't want to. They begin arguing and, due to the additional stress of a poor financial situation, the husband calls his wife several names before storming out of the house to go for a drive and calm down. After a drive to the local store to cool off while buying milk, the husband returns where he apologizes to his wife and they sit and talk about their money situation.

**Example Two** – Despite being engaged for four years, Jason and Jemma haven't made plans yet to marry. Jason constantly accuses Jemma of cheating without any basis and has forbidden her from having a private Facebook account or lock on her phone. He constantly checks her stuff to see if she's messaging anyone, and he has accused her of flirting with the guys at work. As a result of all the accusations, Jemma has quit her previous job and works from home as a part time babysitter. Jason now makes more money and has taken control of more financial decisions because of it.

**Example Three** – Tina just turned twenty-one and went out for a night with her friends and family to celebrate being able to legally drink. After a few cocktails Tina and her boyfriend of three years get in an argument because she thinks he was attracted to some other young female patrons at the bar. He insists that he wasn't but she won't listen to him. Upset, she calls a taxi home and waits outside for it to arrive.

The boyfriend, enraged at her storming out of the bar, follows her and tries to get her back inside. He grabs her arm but she pulls away. Angrier, he grabs her arm again and pulls her with a stronger grip. She screams at him to stop and tries to push off but he hits her across the face.

Startled by the commotion from outside, the friends and family come out to see why someone screamed. The boyfriend apologizes to them all saying they both had too much to drink and that she was far too drunk. Tina, on the other hand, is too stunned and afraid to say anything and doesn't mention the situation to her family or friends.

Now, as you can see, the three situations are vastly different, yet all of them described a scene of abuse that happened in a relationship. If a situation such as what was described in the first example occurred, where a husband was simply lashing out verbally and it was a very rare occurrence that was discussed afterwards, the cessation of the relationship is likely not necessary. This is especially pertinent if it is a marriage, where a long term commitment was made.

On the other hand, examples two and three are definitely instances where leaving the relationship is the best and safest route to take. Example two is coercive control and can be the start of a potentially physically abusive relationship. Nonetheless, it still features abuse that is unacceptable. The fact that Jemma was forced to leave her job due to her fiancé's insecurities is outrageous. Additionally, not letting her have male friends, refusing to allow her to have a private life and phone, are all signs of a manipulator and abuser. Jemma should call off the engagement immediately and break it off with Jason. She has allowed the power in the relationship to shift completely to him in an attempt to ease his insecurities. Unfortunately, situations such as these, where they are not physically abusive, often become physical over time and can be incredibly dangerous.

Example three is a great example of a single instance of abuse. Tina sadly doesn't speak up immediately when it occurs and the boyfriend displays a very worrisome quality in that he minimizes the situation by talking about how intoxicated Tina is. Pushing the blame onto Tina for the instance occurring, and also refusing to admit it happened are all signs that this single instance of abuse won't be the last time it occurs.

All too common, women accept that they're the ones who "caused" their partner to hit them. All too frequently, abusers degrade their victims, minimize situations, and perpetuate the abuse cycle. Letting someone get away with emotional or physical abuse even the one time is opening up a doorway to a horrible, dangerous, and life threatening relationship that can and will turn sour.

So, as you can see, there are situations where some mild forms of abuse are not exactly cause to completely cease the relationship. Some people have incredibly high standards and will have a zero tolerance on verbal, emotional, physical, and financial abuse. However, name calling is a form of abuse that is practiced by many people in relationships and often only occurs during heated arguments. Ensuring that these mild forms of abuse are immediately addressed through calm discussion is crucial to the prosperity of the relationship as a whole. On the other hand, when continued emotional and verbal abuse occurs, or an instance where physical abuse happens, then ceasing that relationship immediately is absolutely essential! As I mentioned previously, one of my missions in life is to help stop the perpetuating cycles of abuse.

Lend your support by joining The 'No Strikes' Campaign today. Let's work together to nip abuse in the bud before other victims become enslaved and accepting of it.

Go to: www.MyChoiceMarriage.com/No-Strikes

## Should I Actually Leave My Partner?

If you're having doubts, anxiety, or even reservations of sorts about potentially leaving your partner, then you need to really steel your reserve before committing to a plan of action. An abuser will do everything to ensure that their victims feel alone, pitiful, and helpless when in reality, the abuser wants them all to themselves – much like a dog with a bone. Manipulation and coercion are some of the greatest tools an abuser has and they will do anything to prevent their victims from leaving.

As you've read, an abuser will use a myriad of methods to convince, threaten, and coerce a victim to stay with them. From children, threats of physical violence, control over finances, to even plain degrading, a person who is the victim of abuse in a relationship needs to truly control their wits and have an iron determination before they begin attempting to leave.

First, understand that your abuser is a master manipulator. They'll do anything and despite any of the following, you need to really be prepared to leave them if you want your life to get better:

- The abuser hasn't actually physically harmed their victim but there is a lot of emotional and verbal abuse
- The abuser has not changed at all during the course of the relationship, however they are not seeking help for their abuse

- The abuser will blame the victim constantly for reasons why abuse happens
- The abuse is made fun of in a way that the victim feels as if it's not serious or really an issue
- The abuser will constantly pressure their victims to stay with either coercion or intimidation
- The abuser will not be physically aggressive or abusive when the victim becomes passive.
- There were only mild and excusable bits of abuse (keep in mind that NO abuse is excusable!)

Once you've realized how conniving, manipulative, and controlling your abuser is, you can begin working towards leaving them by setting up a plan. Bear in mind that you will need to be careful who you share it with. Some loved ones, though well meaning they may give you advice that is said out of ignorance or that serves them.

*There were times when I shared tiny snippets with those I respected and looked up to. Most of them encouraged me to stick it out because God will turn things around. That caused me to shut down even more.*

*In the last few months before I left, I prayed a particular prayer frequently. This was that God's name be glorified in my husband. One day however I decided to stop praying like this. In fact I actually stopped because I felt that I knew what the outcome would be. This was that my husband would change miraculously and I would finally be with the happy and loving man that I expected him to be. My heart was now beginning to say "Lord let your will be done!"*

*After one such heart-felt declaration, late one night I went to bed but I was woken up suddenly by a voice. This said clearly and simply "it's time to go Norva".*

*I was going to go ahead and apply to study abroad. I could not tell him because he had warned me many times before of the repercussions. If I left he would find me and kill me! His message was clear - under no circumstance would any other man have me!*

*So what did I do? I went ahead and applied for schools abroad and started making plans to improve myself. What I ensured was that I did not go around telling others what I was doing because I did not want him to know or have an idea of what was going on. All I knew was that I had to plan well and that I should take the important items that I would need.*

*In this situation what I learnt was that even though I had hoped that things would change, like his attitude and our relationship, I needed freedom. I needed to be free in my mind and then in my actions. It wasn't about changing him it was about changing me. I could only change by first of all taking responsibility for the things that I do and the things I do not do. That was it.*

# Deciding The Best Time to Leave Your Abusive Relationship

Accepting the fact that your partner is abusive and you need to leave them can be a difficult decision for many people to take. No one wants a relationship to fail – in fact most people stay with someone because they wish to build a life with them and be happy. Unfortunately when a relationship does fail and a person does become abusive then there is no other alternative than to leave.

Now, a common misconception is that if someone is abusive, then you should leave immediately. In reality this is hardly recommended – especially if you're do not feel financially, emotionally, or physically able to.

Since abusers have a habit of isolating their victims, demoralizing them, and ruining their self-esteem, setting up a game plan to leave is often the best way for most people to safely and securely get out of an abusive relationship.

## The Six Month Rule

Generally, the sooner you're able to get out of the relationship, the better. If you continue putting off leaving your abuser, or you continue finding excuses to stay, then you're likely not in the right mindset needed to truly leave them. Since an abuser is going to try and convince you in countless ways to come back, you truly need to ensure that you're dedicated to leaving them, that you realize it's the best decision, and that you know nothing they can and will say is going to change your mind.

Make sure that no matter what, you have a six month deadline for your plan of action. Once you make a deadline for leaving, you can set in place everything you need to help ensure your departure from the relationship will be a permanent one. This means that you need to look into reconnecting with friends and family, ensuring that you've got a job and a place to go to, and that you've got the appropriate authorities aware of your situation so that you can call on them within a minutes' notice and receive help if you need it.

Six months is far longer than most people need to successfully leave their abusive partner. However, if you have dependents it will take a bit more planning for the ideal situation, which is why you need to allot for time. If your children need to finish the school year, or you need to wait until their grandparents come back from winter vacation so you can leave the children with them, then allot for a slightly longer time frame.

## Leaving Immediately

Planning ahead allows victims of abuse to appropriately gather their things and get in the right mindset, however sometimes a plan to leave just doesn't work out as it should. Furthermore, sometimes it is absolutely unadvisable for someone to continue to reside with an abuser for one more second. These situations are drastic, messy, complicated, and often involve authorities to help ensure a safe transition.

Leaving immediately may be necessary if you feel:

- That your life is in danger
- That you're going to be seriously injured
- That your children or pets may be in harm's way
- Or that any outside family members may be in immediate harm

When people become violent, it is essential that the situation be left immediately. You don't want to wait until it's too late. Becoming an unfortunate statistic that proves, yet again, that homicide in relationships is far too common especially when abuse is involved is something you don't want to do! Additionally, if you have children, you have an absolute priority and dedication to them to ensure they are safe and well. If you feel that they, or yourself, are in immediate danger then no earthly belongings or money is worth being around the abuser a second longer.

Calling the police to assist you as you leave ensures that someone is there to moderate the situation while you gather your essentials. You will also get help to contact the appropriate helpful organizations in your area. In most if not all these reactive cases, calling them may be one of the best decisions you can do. In civilised societies the police take domestic violence and abuse very seriously because it is something they deal with on a regular basis. They know how to help protect victims, how to ensure that the abuser never goes near a victim again, and how to help get a victim in touch with agencies and support groups vital to the recovery process.

Keep in mind, that there are so many people out there to help you, even if you feel abandoned by your friends and family. No one respectable and loving wants to see you hurt or suffering, so allowing it to go on any more is unacceptable. You deserve more out of life and there are people out there willing to protect you and guide you so you can get back on your feet, become the strong and empowered person you truly are on the inside.

Key
Principle

The longer you put up with the unhealthy behaviour,

the more unpleasant, damaging and long-term

the effects will be for you. Decide

that you are leaving.

CHAPTER 8

# BEGINNING THE

# THINKING AND PLANNING PROCESS

*"It takes the same amount of determination to stay in*
*abuse as it does to leave. Now it's up to you.*
*You determine your fate."*

☞ **Author** ☜

**Beginning the mental process; it starts on the inside**

*Many times my ex said to me that silence gave no one a clue as to what one's*
*next move would be. Well come to think of it, he was actually drumming it into*

*my head so much to the point I had to adopt the same mind set so as to be able to free my mind followed by my body.*

*Whenever I started thinking about how I would get away, I became nervous and I could not see how I would succeed. I did not believe that I should leave because of this feeling I had about judgment by Christian brethren. I felt that they would judge me as being wrong for leaving. The truth was that I was advised that I should not worry about his threats since he would not carry them through. That was before he marked my neck with his army hunting knife!*

*When I decided that I was going to leave I saw it all happening in my mind. The next thing I did was to inform those whom I trusted. The people who knew of my plans first were a couple of my close family members because I knew I could trust them completely. I then started making two kinds of plans- long term plans and plans in case of a crisis - that is if I had to leave impromptu.*

*As his erratic behaviour and threats hit the roof, I had to pretend that I wasn't being affected at all but the truth was that it was affecting me. Practicing how to keep my composure was something that I had to keep on doing since I knew that it would all end soon : the pulling, the obscenities; poking my chin as he told me the most horrific words, then to suggest sex, followed by him starting the whole process again.*

*The lesson I learnt here is that when you have a positive goal there will always be distractions, insults and all other forms of abuse. Even though it may be hitting your core, having your goal and working through your process makes it feel less hard hitting. The reason this happens is because of your focus; you are focused on the best outcome. I also learnt that at times one needs to pretend; keep things to oneself or simply tell a faithful few. This is not just because you want to survive but because you want to overcome!*

Leaving an abuser is an incredibly difficult thing to do and is a process that needs to be completed step by step. While leaving an abusive relationship where you have been physically or mentally harmed does take some time, you can prepare yourself during the process knowing that your future is going to be bright and full of happiness. You will begin to feel lighter once you've released yourself from the weight of the abuser!

Before you begin severing connections with the abuser, you need to do a few other things first. Below is a list of the key items you need to take care of during the planning stages of your separation with your abuser.

## Change Your Mindset

An abuser degrades their victim so that the victim feels they are not worthy of happiness, a better life, or cannot get anyone who will treat them with the respect they deserve. This long term emotional damage wreaks havoc on a person's self-esteem and can demoralize a victim. When someone is completely demoralized it makes it almost impossible for them to leave their abuser which, unfortunately, is exactly how the abuser wants them to feel.

To begin throwing off those chains, you need to gain back your own self-respect and at least a drop of self-confidence that you can successfully and safely leave this toxic relationship. This can be done in many ways:

1) Look at yourself each morning in the mirror and pick out three things you love about yourself. Never focus on anything bad. Never let anything the abuser says get in your head. Look at your face, your body, and your physical features. Also look inside yourself and find your strengths and traits that are positive. Each

day, look at yourself and tell yourself how great you are, remind yourself of your talents and your skills, and boost your self-confidence slowly and surely each day. You may feel silly doing this at first but over time the messages will sink in and replace those negative thoughts that the abuser has instilled in you!

2) Look at your abuser and think to yourself that this is not the person you love. You love the 'idea' of a fictitious version of them, which sorry to say is just not there. You want them to change into this loving and caring person who treats you wonderfully all of the time but that's NOT what they truly are. You don't love the abuser. You may care for them but you need to look and remind yourself over and over again that this is not a loving relationship and they are not what you want, or for that matter need in life!

3) Tell yourself every day that your abuser does not truly love you. If they did would they hurt you? Would they call you names and physically harm you? Someone who loves another person unconditionally and to the end of time would NEVER do that. Your abuser is just telling you exactly what you want to hear so you'll stay with them. Don't believe their lies. Tell yourself morning, afternoon, and evening several times "(partner's name) does not love me." Over and over again. You deserve better. Stop believing their lies!

4) Embrace that you are not alone. There is a God who wants to help you if you ask him to. I have experienced his guiding power many times in my life. The key is that I have to choose to listen and so do you. It doesn't take a long fancy prayer. You can simply say 'Lord I have had enough, show me what to do so that I can live a happy fulfilled life. Thank you for hearing my prayer and answering,

amen.' You need to then believe that your prayer has been answered and follow the leading.

5) Therapy – sometimes it's impossible for victims to go see a therapist or a counselor about the abuse that is taking place. If, however, you are able to meet up with someone and schedule a regular therapy session you can benefit immensely from the help they provide. They can offer you tools to boost your self-confidence, ways to really help instill a sense of purpose and dedication in you and also ways to help you get the strength to finally leave your partner. These are all things a professional therapist or counselor can help you achieve! Equally, if your abuser is too controlling, it may not be worth the risk because you will be gone from their sight for certain times and it may trigger their suspicions!

I will not advocate that you just go to your religious leader. Many of them have no formal training in how to genuinely help you, they will be answering based on their belief. I will advise that you take a close look at your leader's strengths and most of all the doctrine that they preach on a regular basis. Feel free to ask them their stance on marriage and divorce. Once you hear radical or sweeping statements like, 'divorce is wrong, marriage is for life or no matter what, with your creator things will work out for your marriage, those are triggers to run a mile.

Unfortunately, I have not just experienced personal abuse but have had many family members and friends go through the same. Some of them have decided to stick it out. In some situations they have knowingly been taking it for over a decade. They let me know that they admire my actions, but do not feel like they can do the same. They have convinced themselves that staying is in their best interest, especially because they are not yet mentally ill or dead due to their abuse. Recently a former childhood friend left her abusive partner and went back to her mother's house. To her family's amazement and disapproval, she was convinced by her priest to go in for marital counselling with her partner, so she went. While there, they allegedly got into a heated debate. The priest called a time out so she took that time to go to the washroom, leaving her husband and the priest in the room. Within minutes her enraged husband followed her to the bathroom, where he strangled her to death and escaped. My point is this, an abuser is not someone to take for granted. You know what you experience in the relationship and how it makes you feel. Do not assume that you have seen all of their rage and do not wait around or put yourself in a position to experience it.

## Begin Looking for Work

Most of the time an abuser will control their victim by refusing to allow them to work, or restricting their income in some way. If you're not in a job currently, then you need to find a way to get an income for when you do leave. This will help boost your confidence as well as allow you to get onto your feet faster and not feel the need to go back with your partner. Looking for work can be difficult, however speaking with a local support group or organization can lead you into the right direction for a plethora of jobs both full time and part time that can suit your needs!

## Gather All The Numbers of Relevant Organisations

This is an important step because you need to have everything at the ready in case something happens. If, all of a sudden, your abuser finds out you're planning to leave them and you have to rush out of the house, you will need to have a handy paper with local agencies numbers on it so you can see them and get the help you need! Additionally, when you do need support or you do need financial aid, help getting a place to stay, or even assistance with keeping your abusive ex turned stalker at bay, then you're going to want to have all of the information at the ready. There are tons of hotlines and local organizations that, once you get in touch with them, can guide you in the right direction and give you a multitude of additional numbers and contact information for help!

Unless you are somewhere with a corrupt police force, you need to also notify your local police department or law enforcement agency about your desire to leave.

I would strongly recommend that you privately seek legal advice so that you will get clear on your rights and what protection orders can be put in place for you and your children. The more knowledge and advice you can get in your favour the better. In some countries and jurisdictions you may even be entitled to get free legal advice and support, because you are a victim of abuse. In addition, see if you can possibly have a police officer with you during the time you will be officially moving out the house, to prevent any harm coming to you, your children or your possessions when you are ready to leave!

## Read About Other Abuse Victims Online

Feeling as if you're alone can make you lose focus and determination, however reading success stories of other abuse victims can empower and educate you on what to do. There are millions of men and women who have been victims of abuse and successfully left the relationship. Some have had a range of problems with their ex's and they may be able to help guide you in the right direction as to what to do in certain situations. Reading about others either online at forums or on blogs is a great way to connect yourself with the rest of the community and to bring you from your world of isolation back where people are there and willing to help! For supportive information and inspirational quotes on a regular basis as you take this courageous step to your freedom 'Like' and comment on our Facebook Fan Page.

Go to: https://www.facebook.com/MyChoiceMarriage

## Connect With a Trusted Person

Another key thing to preparing for your eventual split with your abuser is to connect with a couple of trusted people. You want to avoid connecting with friends and family members, just because they are your relatives; it must go beyond that to trusting their wisdom and respecting their judgment. Especially if you've been isolated from them for a while, it can easily arouse suspicions in your partner and someone can begin spreading rumours about your plan, causing huge problems for you. Instead, try to find a professional you trust to help. These professionals can be a support worker at a local advocacy agency who is designated to help you, or it could be a teacher from the school you've gone to in the past and you've kept in touch with. Either way, connecting with someone and letting them know about your situation and your desire/plan to leave is vital. This way they can not only watch out for you and make sure that you communicate with them regularly and are not harmed but they can also help connect you to important agencies in the local community.

There are usually support systems in place within local communities and they will help you. Finding the right person to reach out to is sometimes difficult, especially if your trust has been broken in the past. Though it may not initially feel like it, there are so many people willing to help you. All you need to do is just ask! Getting in touch with a professional or trusted individual is absolutely vital and you'll be able to finally confide and get advice on the specific situation you're going through. Don't be afraid to finally open up and tell someone about the abuse you're suffering from because no one can help you if you don't let them know! When I opened up about my decision to leave, I informed two totally trustworthy family members that I was certain will not share the information but support my decision. Next, two weeks before I left, I told a friend. One of my siblings found out because the British High Commission telephoned my mother's house asking for me while I wasn't there. I then sat with my siblings, explained to them the situation and insisted that the information absolutely should not be shared with anyone. The last two days I told a few close friends and an acquaintance. Finally, on the day of my departure I shared limited information with a couple other people. Sadly, I wasn't aware of any organisations in my local area or country that could help me. In fact a couple weeks earlier my ex was so abusive one night that I called the local police who never showed up.

I felt sad that I couldn't be more forthcoming with information to people I spoke to, especially my loved ones. I was in survival mode and felt that I shouldn't take chances with my life by divulging information freely. I did hurt some people's feelings by not mentioning to them that I was leaving. But having close relationships didn't count in my mind, just doing everything with wisdom so that I make it out alive. Those who truly loved me totally understood when they found out and to this day they continue to be very supportive of me.

I made the almost ill-fated mistake of opening up to a Christian neighbour in the late night before the day that I left. He was a local taxi driver and we got talking as I travelled in his car that night about ten or eleven. Around six o'clock in the morning I heard a car horn, when I looked out it was the driver who came to my ex husband. As they spoke outside I was filled with fear and began to pray and muttered to myself, 'this guy will get me killed'. After their brief conversation my ex husband returned inside, "what did he want?" I tried to keep a smile on my face while I kept my distance. "He invited me to a crusade at their church," he replied. "Wow, why did he come so early in the morning", I asked. My ex husband explain that he said he felt led to come and didn't want to forget as the day progressed. After that incident I did not feel safe to stay around much longer so I took the first chance I got, which was within thirty minutes of the incident; my husband briefly stepped out and I left for good.

## Keeping Your Decision to Leave a Secret

Aside from deciding to leave your partner, keeping your decision a secret so you can make all of the necessary plans without any hassle or fear is going to be the most difficult thing. Staying in an abusive relationship is absolutely out of the question; however it's during the process of leaving when an abuser can become increasingly violent, unpredictable, and aggressive. It is absolutely crucial to ensure that you do not clue in your partner in any way. This means you need to avoid the following:

- Change in behaviour – If you begin acting more assertive, confident, outgoing, or different in any way then you can cue in your abuser and put them on guard. If their suspicions are roused you will find it far more difficult to leave without a confrontation! Act as passive and meek as possible to avoid any confrontations!

- Reaching out to family/friends that are close to your abuser or like to gossip or simply very talkative – Another massive action to avoid when preparing to leave is speaking carelessly to many family or friends. Most people may look at this and be confused, however the chances of your partner finding out you're communicating with your family or friends again is very high. This can also spill the beans on your plan to leave and you may find that your family and friends also are on good terms with your partner.

So it can be increasingly difficult. Choose wisely who you communicate with, like a trusted professional who not only is familiar with abusive relationships but is impartial in a way that they can help you to the fullest and never have contact with your abuser. Limit family to five or less who are true brethrens.

- Leaving numbers or info about – always make sure that you've hidden not only this book but the numbers of contacts in the community available to help you. If your abuser knows where you might end up going, then he/she can stalk you there and can cause serious problems for you when you're in the process of attempting to break communication with them and leave the relationship. Always be incredibly careful to hide all of your information and safely store it away so they don't find anything!

# Your To-Do List

Based on the things I did in my preparation to leave my abusive ex husband and other research that I have done on this topic, I have assembled a list of things that I believe will help in both your mental and physical preparation. Again, this information should only be shared with one or two very trusting individuals. The list is in no particular order as I believe that they are all equally important. Likewise, this is not a definitive list, but a guideline that you can add to. You should consider carefully where you put this list for safe keeping and how easy it will be for you to access it when necessary. Having said that please bear in mind that this list is for best case scenario, which is if you have the chance to properly prepare before you leave your abuser and this toxic relationship for good. Remember that if you are in imminent danger or feel unsettled in any way, pay attention to that feeling. In that case you should just get out of the house and away from your partner as soon as possible. The whole aim of everything in this book is for you to get away from your abuser. With God's help and guidance follow your intuition, so you can do that safely.

## The list:

- I would suggest you have at least a plan to where you can go.
- Have the contact person's full details for each of the safe places.
- Set up a new and exclusive email address that only you know to store evidence and information of details like incidents, including photos.
  - o  People tend to forget stuff when they are in a rush, so this data base will help
  - o  Never save the password or keep it open on any computer. Always close and logout after you have finished
- Recognise the triggers to your abuser's enraged behavior and to the best of your ability try to avoid being in that scenario.
- Know the phone numbers to your local police, doctor, women's shelter and maybe a place of worship.
- If you telephone a number for help, dial another number immediately after and erase the number in case your abuser hits redial.
- Know what to do if you are injured.
  - o  You should go to an emergency room or your doctor
  - o  Report what happened to you
  - o  Ask that they document your visit
- Try to keep a journal of all the violent incidences. Include:-
  - o  Dates
  - o  Abusive events
  - o  Threats made to you
  - o  What you did in each situation, e.g. if you got injured, went to the emergency room, you cleaned yourself or you told someone

- Keep any evidence of physical abuse, such as:-
  - o  Pictures of any injuries
  - o  A record or picture of the item/s used
- Make a plan for if you need to quietly escape. Know how and where you will get away.
- Make a plan for your children. Include and remember:-
  - o  If they are responsible enough share it with them.
  - o  Consider how close the relationship is with them and the abuser before you divulge important information.
  - o  Only tell them exactly what they need to know in a timely manner
  - o  If necessary, identify a safe place for them to reside temporarily
  - o  Teach them what they can do to stay safe
  - o  Instill in them that they should not to try to protect you as they may get hurt in the process
- Practice the escape, and where appropriate also run through it with your children.
- If you drive you should make it a habit of backing your car into the garage or driveway if you have one, and keep it fuelled.
- Hideaway an extra set of car keys in a special spot.
- Do research into getting a restraining order
- Set money and essentials aside specifically for whichever date that you are leaving:-
  - o  Ask your advisor, friend or family members to hold some money for you.
  - o  Give the person a small packed bag of essential and a full charged phone that is switched off.
  - o  Instruct them to periodically take the phone out and top up the charge.

Below are two lists of items that you should try and locate, in preparation for the day you leave (based on my own experience):-

## Will be great to have

- Another phone with sim card number
- An extra set of keys
- IDs
- Birth certificates
- Social security cards
- Health insurance card
- Medications
- Banking information
- Money
- Credit cards
- marriage license (certificate)
- clothes for yourself and your children
- shoes
- Take essentials and some food for the long term and for the journey
- car title

## Other things to consider taking (these are absolutely not essential)

- your verification of social security numbers
- you children verification of social security numbers
- medical records at your home,
- children's school and immunization records,
- insurance information,
- valued pictures, jewellery or
- important personal possessions

- property information (if your name is on the deeds) e.g. titles, deeds, etc

My prayer for you is that armed with your plan, empowered positive attitude, support and God, you will be able to successfully escape the grips of your abusive intimate [slave] master. This is your Time To Go!

Let us help to support you through your journey all the way to your freedom. Join our Secret Facebook Group today.

Go to: https://www.facebook.com/groups/MyChoiceMarriage

Key
Principle

Don't remain a negative statistic; you have great

power and strength within you. Give yourself

the gift of happiness; start

by making a plan

CHAPTER 9

# LEAVING

# THE ABUSIVE RELATIONSHIP

*"It's Time To Go safely by following your plan."*

 Author

### Leaving the abusive relationship: prepare to succeed

*From the time that I felt the urge to leave as quickly and safely as possible, I started focusing not only on leaving but also on how to improve my life. This was especially in the field of academics. I was fed up with being the victim in the closet. I was going to come out the best way I could - that is a better me who was not only safe but was also happy. That included being educated well so that I would not have to depend on a man for anything. I knew that in an environment that was totally different I would have the freedom to learn and to grow.*

*Even while married to my ex, I was inspired to further my education. Part of my inspiration came from seeing particular members of my former school's volleyball team that I was once a part of were now in admirable jobs with excellent wages. It was a pleasant surprise to see myself succeeding in things that I was made to feel that I couldn't achieve when I was young. A good example being that I had attempted GCSE level Mathematics and English Language approximately seven times before only to end up with grades equivalent to C - D. This was not seen as a pass in Trinidad. However, when I decided to focus on my education, it took me just three months of preparation to pass what I had in the past struggled with. For the first time I felt I could accomplish anything but only when I set my mind for success.*

*The more I studied the more my eyes opened to the toxic situation I was in. I was shouting on the inside, 'I'm not going to take this anymore.'*

*I used my ex-husband's regular saying, 'silence gives no one a clue...' to continue to get many things done. When he said it usually a smug evil look on his face accompanied the words. That would sometimes be followed by a finger poke in my neck. Well, my body remained in the relationship way past the time that my mind did. I had had enough.*

*Over the course of about two months I made plans to go. I had to be sure that when I leave I had no reason to come back. That took planning, strategising, some pretending that life was normal and being scared but pushing through the fear. I started to believe in the possibility of happiness once again.*

*At first I was open to the idea of coming back to my husband but that was actually the thought that comes when the victim is already accustomed to being in the trap of whoever speaks. The truth was that no matter how much I accomplished it was never celebrated. My ex-husband always found a reason to belittle me and to show me that I was wasting not only his time but mine too. So that the thought of trying again was in the end short lived by the time I stepped out of the abusive environment.*

For some, the fear of putting all of those carefully made plans into action can be paralyzing. Many victims of abuse often find that, while the abuse is horrific and unbearable at many times, the normality of their situation becomes oddly comforting to them. Don't be lured into staying simply because the uncertainty of change and the fear of not knowing your future frightens you. The truth is that you DO know what your future will be: a bright one without the constant and degrading abuse you've suffered! You don't need to be afraid because while you may be uncertain about exactly what you're going to do afterwards, you are free from the bonds and chains laid on you before!

*Actually, taking the first steps of leaving is the hardest part but it will be the most important step of your life!*

## Preparing Yourself to Actually Leave

So how do you leave? How do you finally buck up the courage to walk out that door with your belongings and children (if you are a parent)?

1.   Listen to motivational and inspirational music

Don't underestimate the power of music, especially in these times where you need motivation and strength the most. Music can bring us to tears, can lift our spirits, and can send us into an angry frenzy depending on what we choose to play! So get some CD's or download some songs and listen away to motivate yourself each day! Packing your things to something motivational and uplifting will really help and will also keep your mind not focused on fear but instead on other things so you'll be far more productive! If you need to steel your resolve then perhaps get some angry metal music playing and rock out! You can really pump yourself up and bring out the fire you need to help you leave your abuser once and for all!

2.   Set up a meeting with someone to leave

You should NEVER leave with your abuser there, instead you need to know their schedule and make sure you leave at a time when they won't be around. Additionally, if you're looking to make sure you actually stick to your plans and leave, then have a trusted person come over and meet you at your place to help you pack. They will be there to ensure you do follow through with your plans, and also help calm you because you will understandably be nervous and anxious about the entire situation!

If you do not have any trusted people you can count on to come to the house and help you get away, then call the non-emergency phone number for the police department and explain your situation. They can help ensure that there is a social worker, or a police officer there to help escort you from your home to your new location. Additionally, they will also be more than willing to get you in touch with individuals and organizations that will assist you on further steps to getting rehabilitated after you leave your partner, and moving on with your life successfully!

3.  Identify the items on your lists and work through

Lists are amazingly helpful because they can provide incredible clarity in situations where all seems lost. In your times leading up to the actual move out date, you need to make lists about why you're leaving and make notes to yourself about how your abuser has never changed when he/she has apologized. When you make clear lists saying what they've done to you and your children if you have any, then you can read over it constantly on the day of leaving, and during the days after you leave, to remind yourself why you should never ever go back or think about giving your abuser a second chance! Next you need to work through the to-do and know where to locate the things. If you can put aside without arousing too much suspicion, do that.

4.  Fake it until you make it

Faking your actions and feelings to your abuser is something you've probably become accustomed to since you've first made the decision to leave. During your planning stages it is crucial for you to constantly put on a façade to your abuser so they believe that you're still the passive victim they've made you into. On the actual day of leaving where you need to pack your things and rush out before your abuser returns, you need to put on a mask of bravery and resilience. Force yourself each and every step of the way because you're going to feel a myriad of conflicting emotions and you need to listen only to those telling you to run as fast and as far as you can from your abuser.

Instead of giving into that seemingly overwhelming amount of fear, or listening to that nagging voice saying "give him/her another chance, things will change" that your abuser instilled into you, you need to remember EVERYTHING horrible that they've done to you and said to you. You need to turn all of that pain that was inflicted onto you into a

127

mask to help you ignore all of the doubts you're feeling. You are never going to change your abuser, and you need to realize it. While you may have doubts now, ignore them and just fake it. Eventually your thinking will change and your mindset will change so that you actually believe it. You'll eventually become stronger and more resilient as you continue faking your way through this ordeal!

## Don't Underestimate Your Abuser

An abuser loves the power and position they are in, so undoubtedly when something threatens that (such as you leaving them), they can often react in a very aggressive and unpredictable manner. Never underestimate your abuser in any way, especially when it comes to the day of your leaving. You need to be on guard the entire time, expect them to be violent (even if they never have been previously), and also expect the worst just so you are prepared fully.

The most dangerous time in an abusive relationship is not during the relationship itself, it's when the abuser is being separated from his/her victim. They fear being exposed and they fear losing the control so they can be incredibly violent and it's exactly why you need to take every precaution necessary. Aside from not cluing them in with attitude changes or by telling friends and family members, who may hint at you leaving your abuser, you can do the following things to ensure a safe transition from your relationship to your new life, and to avoid any unpleasant circumstances in-between:

1.  Keep your children safe

This is a huge priority, especially when you're in a relationship where physical violence took place. Notifying the school authorities, child services, and the police about the physical violence and your intentions to leave with your children (should you have any) is absolutely necessary. You need to make sure that you keep your children away from your abuser because if they are the biological parent, they still have parental rights and can remove them from school without notifying you. If you've taken the proper precautions, then you can make sure that your children are safe and bring them with you to your new or temporary home. From there you need to notify all of the childcare providers and teachers about your abusive partner. Make sure that you have the authority and documents to show the providers they can prevent the other parent from taking the child in any circumstances.

2.  Let two people know on the day of you leaving

Keeping yourself and anyone else involved on the day of you leaving is crucial, so you need to make sure that there are enough people looking after you who understand the situation. Letting at least two people know, whether they're the police, a neighbour, family member, friend, or someone else will ensure that should something happen to one person, the other is able to contact authorities and alert them that there is something wrong and to come check on you.

3.  Develop a code word

While one can only hope a situation doesn't come to it, you need to prepare for the worst. Abusers have been known to become homicidal in certain situations, so you need to make sure that you're prepared for it and have a code system in place to discretely alert someone. Use a predetermined phrase such as "I forgot to get cat food the other day" or "I broke a glass this morning" or something as a way to alert a person of you being in danger should your abuser find out about your plan and be preventing you from leaving. With this set in place your friend or the person you've contacted can then call the police and immediately send help over with the knowledge that you're in harm's way and that your abuser can be acting irrationally.

### 4. Don't arouse suspicions

Last but definitely not least, don't arouse suspicion on the day of your leaving. This means don't turn off your phone if/when your partner goes out because they could easily return home early should their suspicions be provoked. Abusers are very distrustful and alert by nature, so any tiny clue can set them off on a hunt to find the truth – potentially exposing your entire plan and putting you in an incredible amount of danger!

Along with not turning off your phone, you need to make sure that when you are out of the house that you don't answer it when you're in any identifiable locations. This means if you're at an airport, train station, bus station, or something similar and your abuser calls you, don't answer it because they may immediately come looking for you and you'll be placed in danger or your new temporary safe location could be found if they stalk you!

It's absolutely necessary to envision your abuser using any means necessary to not only find out where you are but who you've talked with. This means that on the day of your leaving, you need to wipe every piece of evidence from the house. This means get rid of all papers in the trash you may have crumpled up that had information or numbers on them. Besides that, you should wipe the computer history every time you do research that will help you, especially if you were searching specific locations or organizations. Don't forget to also dial a few numbers on the telephone to ensure that when they go back through the history they can't get the one you last dialled. Small mistakes like those listed above can not only put yourself in extreme danger but can also lead anyone who has helped you into harm's way. Take care to do everything possible while you're in the house and get out on just one trip!

I know that some women make it a point of telling their partner that they are leaving them. In a regular unhappy relationship that is abuse free, it is admirable that you can part ways amicably. On the other hand, I believe that when you are in any type of abusive situation, caution and much thought must be given if you feel the need to boldly tell your abusive partner that you are planning to leave them. Always consider that the nature of an abuser is to control. Therefore, you coming to them with that type of information, says to them that you are undermining their control and authority. When the nature of your toxic relationship involves physical abuse against you, it is even far more important to not disclose your plans to the abuser or other individuals who may let the information of your plans slip.

*I recently heard of an incident that reduced me to tears. It is still being investigated, so all I am about to say comes with the disclaimer of 'allegedly'. A popular female Caribbean Television presenter had 'allegedly' planned to end her marriage. Her name was Marcia Henville[1]. She was born in Britain but for many years she made Trinidad her home, where she excelled as a media personality. Marcia sought divorce advice and hired a lawyer who helped her draw up the documents to be served. The woman lived with her husband and two children aged 16 and 20. At around six o'clock on a Saturday morning Fire officials and police officers were called to their second storey flat because of a fire. Neighbours reported to the authorities and reporters that some of them 'allegedly' heard an argument taking place inside the family home. That was shortly followed by an explosion and fire. The fire was confined to the couple's bedroom where only her body was found. Marcia's husband escaped from a*

*window with minor burns and the children were unharmed. The divorce documents were due to be signed and filed on the following Monday, which was two days after her death. A few days later the autopsy results concluded that the presenter's death was due to being murdered – the cause of death was determined to be blunt force trauma and multiple stab wounds. The only suspect in this case is her husband, who has insisted that there were no domestic issues in their relationship. However, other people who knew the couple claimed that the relationship was 'difficult'.*

My point of sharing this story is that you have to be very careful when planning your leave and never underestimate your abuser. One of the ironies of this tragedy is that Marcia dedicated much of her professional life to helping the oppressed and disenfranchised. She courageously went into Trinidad 'crime hotspots', well known because of the prevalence of drugs and gang warfare, in order to lend her voice to the voiceless of those areas. Marcia's immediate family and former colleagues have decided to turn her social media accounts into a forum for people who are or have been victim to domestic abuse.

You can go to: https://www.facebook.com/MarciaHenville1

## Leave in a Safe Manner

Crucial things you need to do within days of you leaving or just before you leave!

Develop and practice an escape plan – make sure that you know what to do if you get trapped in the house or if your abuser comes home at any point. This means leaving windows unlocked so you can run out, have an emergency bag packed in your car, and also leave the driver side door unlocked so you can quickly escape!

Print off extras – get an extra set of car keys and hide them outside. This way if you have to actually execute your escape plan, and your keys are taken from you, you can still get away to safety and not be trapped!

Locate and get crucial documents – there are certain documents you will need if you are going to start your life over in a new place. This means you will need your social security card (if you're a US citizen), your passport (if you're a foreigner), birth certificate, driver's license, lease documents (if you've signed the lease), and anything else. Also make sure you get the same papers for your children as well so you don't have to run into conflicts when you go to enrol them in a different school for their safety!

Prepare the car – not only should your car be backed up so you can just drive away without having to reverse but you also need to make sure it is fuelled up. This is such a simple yet critical step because you don't want to have to stop just a few minutes away from your abuser's home to refuel! This could lead to you potentially being followed by your abuser!

Instruct your children on the day of departure – do not tell them any time before because little kids, and even teenagers, are not capable of fully understanding the severity of the situation and keeping quiet about the plans. You can easily put them in danger by telling them your escape plans, so it is absolutely crucial to wait until the abuser leaves before telling them, and then instructing them what to do if your abuser comes back. Make sure they know to run out of the house and go to a neighbour's house or somewhere trusted for help rather than wait with you because their safety is paramount. Today most children have mobile/cell phone and if they feel the need to, they could call your abuser or someone connected to them and share that you are leaving with them. To avoid such calls I would suggest that you confiscate their phone until you feel it is safe to return the phone to them. The last thing you need is for your child to lead your abuser right to you. Remember that they may not be keen to leave the familiarity of their home for an unknown existence.

Take your journal and other important documents with you. If you kept a journal or documentation of previous abuse instances, this may be useful as evidence for the courts or police departments should you need to get a restraining order for you and your children. This is absolutely crucial and you should not forget it!

This is an important safety consideration. Whilst the advice is that you take everything you need, including all that has been mentioned above, make absolutely sure that you do not then need to return to the property for anything. This is because you do not want to run the risk of bumping into your abuser with potentially dangerous consequences. Moreover, in taking all that you need resist the urge to clear the house of all its content. This will only serve to aggravate your spouse over and above the shock of you leaving.

A word of caution. Marcia Henville's story and countless others demonstrate what can happen leading up to you leaving your spouse. Do not get into argument or conversation with your abuser before or whilst leaving. It is always wise to move out of the property when your partner is not at home. However, sometimes it is not as straight forward as you might like. In the week prior to your proposed leaving day do try to hold your tongue so you don't help create any unnecessary tension. On the day of your departure in particular avoid any arguments. Furthermore, don't be persuaded to stay because the control and manipulation will only get worse if you do.

## Getting a restraining order – is it necessary?

A restraining order is something that is highly advised for situations where abuse took place, however many victims of abuse don't get one. If you are planning your escape, then obtaining a restraining order is absolutely necessary because you are obviously living in fear of your partner and the abuse you will or have suffered from them. There are many misconceptions about a restraining order, so it is important to understand them. First off, it generally takes forty-eight hours from the initial paperwork filing for a temporary restraining order to be issued. This temporary order will be in effect until a court date is set where a full five year restraining order can be put into place.

Another common mistaken belief is that you can only get one if you've been hit by your abuser before; this is not true at all. A restraining order is set up to prevent victims from violence, harassment, and stalking. This means that you can get one if you feel your abuser may become violent or has threatened you with violence. If you are in the process of leaving, make sure to bring evidence of violence (if there was any previously) with you – these can include holes in the wall from anger, damaged items that were thrown about, or even photos on an old phone or camera from where you suffered physical abuse.

A further misconception is that a police report about violence in the past needs to be made. This is not true at all and means that you can file a restraining order and have it successfully awarded at court even if you've never contacted the police in any way. You will need to back up your claims, however, so make sure if you don't have physical proof of aggression and violence, that you have witnesses testify on your behalf.

Keep in mind that you must never get a restraining order under false pretenses. This is a huge violation of the law and you will get into trouble with the courts and police department if you make false claims.

There is never a need to lie or make up false accusations against your abuser – physical, financial, and emotional abuse is bad enough and you can get a restraining order under normal circumstances if you feel threatened and can prove you actually feel threatened.

[1]http://globalvoicesonline.org/2015/01/27/trinidad-tobago-journalist-marcia-henvilles-murder -shocks-the-nation

Key
Principle

Leaving can be the hardest part, and most

dangerous period but it will be the

most important steps in your life

# CHAPTER 10

# FINANCING YOUR LEAVING

# EVEN IF YOU HAVE NO MONEY

*"An SOS message from the one in need makes it easier*
*for the rescuer to help you."*

☞ **Author** ☜

**Where there is a will there is a way**

*I was now living with an unemployed man who had an excuse for why he quit his job as a police man. He would find reasons to leave the house, normally because he said he had a sure job lined up. The sure job would at times cause him to leave home early in the morning and return home after 10pm at night with no job. This went on for three years, with him getting the odd job at times and having a complaint about why the environment or income wasn't good enough for him to stick it out. Except for the occasions where he brought home some money, we were dependent on my great grand aunt. Now that I had the urge that I had to leave I had to work out where I would get the money.*

*Whether he was supportive of my decision or not I was determined to work as long and as hard as it took to put the money together. I made plans for my daughter to be taken care of by my family during the day and looked for opportunities. As the small ad hoc jobs came my way I had to lie to him about my income. I made sure he didn't have access to the account that it would be deposited into.*

*The national census application process began and as a lactating mother I waited for hours in line to do the exams. As I inched closer to the front of the line in my white shirt, my now engorged breast leaked past my breast pads and soaked my shirt. I smelt like Nefertiti, the Queen of Sheba and Cleopatra after their alleged bath in camels or donkeys milk, minus the rose petals. With my new look I sailed through the written part of the application and had a break before coming back for a face to face interview.*

*During the break I made my way to a friend of my family who lived close by. She loaned me a black thick T-shirt. During my face to face it happened again, luckily for me I kept my composure and the interviewers were none the wiser. I got the job and with that one quarter of the money I needed was secure.*

*I was given a job in the office with was a lot of work and responsibility. One of the field workers decided she had enough and I was given the opportunity to share the job between a colleague and myself. I was now one-third of the way to my financial goal. The census job ran for a few weeks from Monday to Friday. I sometimes had to go in on weekends which made it impossible for me to do any other paid work during that time. I also had to be there for my great grand aunt as it was during this period that my husband disappeared for eleven days. I had to now leave my daughter with my mum as it was impractical to go collect her every night. My day looked something like this – up at 5:30am, ready by 6am, make breakfast for my aunt and myself, and lunch for her, leave house by 6:45am, arrive at work by 7:55am, do admin work till 9am, start field work 9:30am till 3pm, work in office till 10pm, get home by between 12am and 2am (depending on the time it took to get a taxi). Those were some difficult days. I thank God my aunt had a steady flow of friends who would stop by during the day. I was riddled with guilt, especially when she asked me where my husband was. I always answered that he went out.*

*Over the next few weeks, the census ended and I did other odd jobs which brought the finance up to fifty percent. I then had to ask a family member for a loan, which bought me up to ninety-five percent. The last five percent seemed practically impossible to get. That was to cover my transport to the airport and departure tax. I booked the transport by faith and asked if it was alright if he was paid in a few weeks by my mum.*

*On the Sunday morning as I prepared to leave Trinidad, I went to inform one of my spiritual leaders that I was leaving. We prayed together and as I left they took out some money and gave it to me. I began to cry with gratitude. "Do you have all that you need?" I looked at how much I was given. "No!" I replied. Before I could say any more I was told this story " I was told by God to take a certain amount of money from the bank and keep it with me. I put it in my pocket this morning, as I gave you a portion God said it's all for her that's why I asked the question. Here is the rest." The money totalled to all that I needed with a few dollars to spare.*

*I cannot tell you that it will happen for you as it did for me, nor should you want it to. I had some difficult days but I was willing to do whatever I could and trust God to do the rest. He certainly did not fail me.*

Planning for the money to fund your new life should have been part of your previous process. Understandably this may not have been possible if your abuser has control of your bank assets and/or other financial means. Unfortunately, money is needed to get back on your feet but not necessarily to get you out of the situation (I will explain in a bit). Getting the money needed can be done one of several ways. Just think about it really, if someone was holding a gun to your head or your children's head and said "Give me $2,000 or I pull the trigger" you would do absolutely anything possible to get the money including beg, borrow or pawning your personal belongings.

## The Victim Feels Trapped

Whether it's a personal struggle you are going through currently, or it is a story you heard about someone else, you will often hear of a victim staying with their abuser for far longer than they should. Oftentimes victims stay for years, allowing themselves to be abused by their partner. A victim may vow many times to leave. Understand that there are always reasons that prevent them from going. There are many reasons why a victim may feel chained to their abuser, and oftentimes these are imposed by the abuser themselves. Reasons can include children, low self-esteem, lack of transportation, and financial insecurity.

# Breaking The Financial Dependency

Abusers work on creating a situation where their victims are completely dependent on them. They isolate them from friends and family, and then oftentimes make it so they are also financially dependent as well.

One of the first and most crucial steps for an abuser in creating financial dependency in their victims is to tell them to either leave their job or lower their hours. This means that the victim not only is forced to stay home more but they are also earning a lot less income.

Unfortunately when a victim begins to plan their escape, they may feel defeated before even beginning because they lack certain essentials such as: - a car- excess finances for hotel/motel room- a phone- money for food and basic necessities- money for children. Thankfully there is no need to feel defeated. While you may feel as if you have no way of leaving because you have no money and no way of discretely getting money, that is not true!

Below we have over sixteen possible ways for you to get extra money so you can finally leave your abuser and start a new life.

Now at this juncture it is important that I introduce another disclaimer. I am not recommending that you use any of the methods described. I am making you aware about options that you have, that you may or may not have been considering.

## Approach Family Members and Friends

Chances are good that many of the people you are about to approach would have needed financial support at sometime as well. This means that they may empathise with you and once they can afford to, be inclined to help you out. You are one of their own so they should not blame or judge you.

Some family and friends may even know what it's like to be in your situation. You are not the first person to be in an abusive situation but you are a courageous example because you are working toward getting out safely. When you approach family and friends, or anyone else for that matter please keep this perspective in mind.

I believe that you should approach your loved ones to ask for two things, one some financial help; because if you don't ask you won't get. Number two, you should ask for a loan but with a realistic payback time frame. When you are going through a challenging situation it is at times very difficult to make practical decisions, primarily about loans and repayment because you are about to enter unknown circumstances. Asking for and receiving financial assistance, no matter how small the amount means that you have a bit of breathing space to make some key decisions that will affect your safety and survival. So go and ask with confidence.

Remember that when you ask the answer could be yes or no. Try not to take a no as a rejection of you. The person may not be in a financial position to offer the help to you. Having said that, make sure you also ask about a loan.

Whether it's close family, friend, acquaintance or anyone else, for that matter people who give loans care about one thing — getting their money back as promised. You have to be very clear and practical about why you want the money, so be prepared to share a bit about your situation with them. For your safety think long and hard about who you are asking; whether they are trustworthy with the information about your predicament. The last thing you need is for word to get back to your spouse that you are making plans to leave. There will be some people who don't really care about what you are going to do with the money. They just want their money back as you promised. Ask for a loan that you can payback in a year, certainly no earlier than six months. Even if you think you know where the money would come from to repay the loan, it is better to ask with a longer than realistic time frame and then you pleasantly surprise the person by paying back earlier than they expected. Remember that after the dust is settled these are the people that you want to continue having a great relationship with.

Before you ask anyone for a loan get out a piece of paper and start to jot down the names of people you want to ask, who you believe you can trust and who might be willing to give you a loan. At the top of the list, write down the names of people who are most able to make the loan and who you believe have the willingness to do so.

Bear in mind that even if you are sure the person at the top of the list is going to happily assist you, no questions asked, keep adding names to your list. You never really know what someone is going to do until they do it. I would suggest that you make a list of at least 25 people; the larger your list the better. This will help in two ways – you won't pin your hopes on any one person and you will be able to approach each person with a more positive attitude. Again you don't want a negative answer to make you more frustrated, nervous or depressed than you may already be feeling.

Once you've completed your list, look it over and consider each person's personality, character, morality and if they have a habit of gossip etc. You should sort the list with those who best meet all your criteria.

Before you make contact with anyone on your list make sure that you have a clear figure in mind that you will like to get and have a plan or explanation of how you propose to pay back the loan to them. I would also suggest that you offer to pay a small sum of interest; depending on the total amount borrowed; it could be a fixed sum or a percentage. This will make the person you approach more willing to assist you.

Write down a one year plan and include how you intend to gain finance as soon as it is possible. Do not borrow too much over what you believe you would need to leave and get set up for the next 3 months or so.

Impress your friends and family by not coming across as a mere victim but an empowered individual who is taking back control of his or her life. Show them that you have been giving the situation much thought and that you are serious about making good of your life and future. Passion and conviction goes a long way but remember to be sincere and truly work towards making good on your commitment of repayment. If it means you have to take on extra work in the future then do that. This should be so, no matter where you obtain the loan from.

It is important that when you speak to your loved ones do so without expectations. You may not know what that person is facing on a personal or financial level; so don't assume that a "no" means they don't care about you or don't want to help you. Be cordial and appreciative if you are given anything, be it financial help or nothing. If you are feeling nervous about asking people close to you for money you are not alone. It can be nerve wrecking just thinking about it, it is said that fear is being uncomfortable of the feeling you get or expect to get. Try to ask yourself in the mirror at least 10 or more times. The important thing is being authentic. Getting a loan from people close to you doesn't have to be complicated or a stressful experience. Once you are real, have the right attitude and be open to any answer, the process just may help you get closer to your loved ones too.

## Go to The Bank and Apply For a Loan

Getting a loan is quite a simple process and often can be completed within the day if you make an appointment with an advisor. A loan can be granted for a few hundred dollars, clear to several thousand.

Unfortunately your credit score and income often plays a part in the approval process. If your spouse made you quit your job, or made you drop your hours, this could prove troublesome. Thankfully, there are often ways to still get approval.

A loan advisor can sometimes speak with management and override the disapproval for a loan. This can be done in extenuating circumstances, so you need to be prepared. Bring in police documentation, proof of recent and previous work, plus proof that your hours were reduced. Explaining to the advisor that you are using the money to leave your spouse and showing them the adequate documentation can overturn the decision for your loan. You may not be able to get thousands of dollars but a few hundred can be more than sufficient to get you settled for a few months.

A great tip is to go to a bank and get an actual loan, avoid those 'scammy' payday loans that charge exorbitant amounts of interest rates. These types of loans will only serve to put you in debt and create more problems where you don't need them.

## Get a Credit Card

Another way to have access to money for leaving your partner is by getting a credit card. Credit cards are much like loans although they often have higher percent of interest repayment. Fortunately, you can frequently find credit cards with six months zero interest. This allows you to easily use the full amount on the credit card and have half of a year to pay it back before ever having to pay interest. If you already have a credit card, consider requesting a higher limit so you have more money.

Unfortunately if you have a credit card in both you and your spouse's name, it's advisable that you completely forego using that card.

147

Additionally, if you already have a card that you are going to use and request a higher limit on, make sure that your spouse does not know the login information so they can track where you are and what you are spending your money on.

An important note is to always make sure to change your passwords, security questions, pin numbers, and login details. Do not make any password the same as a previous one and do not use simple security questions. Also make sure to contact all of your providers and tell them to not give out your details over the phone to your spouse because you're leaving them.

## Get Funding From a Local Organization that Helps Victims

Many victims of abuse do not truly realize how much help is available to them. There are so many organizations out there that offer housing, counselling, food, clothing, and money to abuse victims. Simply contacting your local organization and explaining your situation can help connect you with an entire network of people who are able to help. Getting advice from someone on leaving, having a trusted confidant available to speak to, and securing funding and housing for when you do leave will help you successfully and safely break away from your abusive spouse for good. If you don't know who to call you can either Google the term 'help for domestic violence victims', call your local police or contact your borough council.

## Become A Live-In Care Giver

If you are mentally and physically up to it, there is a great option of becoming a care-giver to an elderly or disabled person. This is a win-win situation: you will be in a live-in job thus taking care of accommodation, food, utilities, etc whilst the individual in need of assistance gets the companionship that they need, enabling them to remain in their own residence. You may be asked to do tasks ranging from cooking and household chores to simply being there as a security for them. You may also have opportunities to chat and watch television. Depending on your role and duties there is a possibility of being paid on top of the inherent benefits. Some placements will allow you to come with your children but that may take a bit more searching to find a home where that is allowed. To start your research search online for 'live-in care jobs', put in the geographic area you would like to live in.

## Sell Valuables Including Jewellery or Heirlooms

It can be so hard to part with certain heirlooms and items that you may not even consider pawning them as an option. It is important to understand that absolutely nothing is worth more than your life. If your grandmother passed down her wedding ring to you, or if your mother gave you a precious gold necklace, just think about how much they loved you and know that they would have given anything for you not to be in an abusive relationship. Do not feel guilty about pawning something to leave. Material items are not worth your life. If, however, you are simply too attached to something, you can see about buying the item back AFTER you have left. Certain pawn shops can allow you an allotted amount of time to pay them back (usually at a higher price). However, make sure that you are financially secure enough to do so.

## Get a Loan Against Your Car

A great way to quickly and securely get a sum of money to leave your abusive spouse is to get a loan against your car. A loan against your car works because you have equity in it, and even if you do not own your car outright you can still obtain the loan if you have paid off enough of the value of your car. Essentially you will put the title of your car up as collateral for the loan. This means that if you do not pay off your loan, you are forfeiting your vehicle. Make sure that the car is only in your name; else you may wind up in more financial problems related with your abusive spouse. If you wish to obtain a loan against your vehicle, then there are many ways to go about doing so. First is to find out how much your vehicle is worth and then to find a lender. Many different companies allow you to use online tools to input the vehicle information (such as the VIN, model, make, year, condition, etc) and how much you owe on it if you still have it on loan. These companies will then give you a quote on how much of a loan you can get and allow you to begin applying for that loan. Keep in mind that if you default against the loan then the lender will then have the ability to repossess your car. Additionally, loans against your car are often given out at a higher interest rate so it is something to consider before going through this route.

## Speak to Your Boss And Get a Pay Cheque Early

If you have a job then one of the most effective ways of securing extra money is by simply speaking to your boss. Explain to your boss about you needing to get a pay cheque early and they will likely do everything they can to assist you in leaving your spouse. People are willing to help you and you'll find that there are many who will go out of their way to ensure you are able to successfully leave your spouse. There are several ways you can get paid early. Firstly, you can ask your boss to be paid for the work you had done up to that day of the month. However, bear in mind that the amount you will get will depend on the time of the month of your request. Secondly, and particularly if the first option is not viable, you can ask your boss for a wage advance. These are workable solutions, however if you are still tight on finances you ought to consider approaching your boss to discuss any other viable options. If you do end up getting a wage advance do try and negotiate a favourable repayment plan that does not overstretch you. Another alternative is that you request the use of the deposit that you may have made when you first join the company. With some employers when one first starts, the company hold the first payment. This is then used as security in the event that you break something or there is a need to use that payment. By communicating sensitively with your boss you may be able to obtain that cheque. Bear in mind, that whilst the amount of money may not be huge it should still ensure that you can cover the costs of basic expenses such as food, clothing, fuel, and housing.

## Rent Out Your Spare Space for storage etc

Whether you are the one moving out of the house you currently occupy or your abusive partner, a great option for extra cash is to rent out areas in and around your house. The areas can be your driveway, garage, parking space, garden or shed space as storage. Renting out your spare space can be very lucrative especially in busy areas close to the transport links like airports, bus stations, metro and train stations where parking is usually a problem. Other vicinities where parking is expensive like malls and city centres, large amusement parks and conference venues etc. are also great for rendering this service because you can charge a more favourable price. For things like sport and music/concert many people are even happy to camp out in your garden. When it comes to needing storage space I have personal experience. I went in search of sheds, attics and cellars and I have now been renting two sheds for the past four years.

Be sure to do your research and carry out the appropriate checks. Ask as many questions as possible particularly before letting anyone into your home as you will be dealing with complete strangers who have the potential to not be what they claim to be. For more peace of mind it may be better to do it through an agency, there are many online. In addition, whether you are storing possessions for people or housing them temporarily, be sure to inform your home insurance company so that you will know if it will affect your policy and by how much.

## Rent out Your External Vehicle Space for Company Advertising

If you do a lot of driving on a weekly basis or you park your car in a well lit busy area, some companies will be happy to use the space on your vehicle bodywork for advertising their products or services. This is a prime advertising spot similar to newspapers, billboards and television. For years this service was provided by bus companies and airplanes but now it has been extended to almost any size of personal vehicle. You can host advertising from small panels placed on the sides of the car to a customised wrap, which covers the entire circumference. What you are paid will depend on your vehicle size and how much of the vehicle is covered in the advert. You can search online for more information about doing this.

## Rent out a Room Short Term as living space

This is similar to the above as you are renting out space but this time the individual's will be occupying your home. This can include, attic/ loft, basement/cellar if these are habitable as well as conventional rooms. Therefore, it goes without saying that even more due diligence should be done before inviting anyone into your house. If you have a room with an ensuite washroom you can offer it to a tourist, who will only be in your home for a short period of time. You may be asked to provide general tourist information like great local places to visit, where to eat and spots to avoid.

You can also offer longer term hosting for professionals who may be stationed at a post in your local area for a temporary period. My husband did this when he was in a six-month placement with his job. He came home most weekends as we live two hours from where he was working.

Be sure to do the following before accepting individuals into your home:

- Communicate with each potential guest before hand to be sure that you both feel comfortable with each other.
- Do a police check or at least get some references about the individual and do some digging.
- Check with your state tax office, in some states and countries your income from offering lodging may be tax-free based on how much you are charging. Sometimes the tax-free allowance is capped at a certain amount.
- Again, tell your home insurance company and get advice. In general, contents insurance does not cover the belongings of visitors or lodgers therefore additional cover may be required.

It is preferable to do it through an agency so that they can also to checks on your behalf. It will cost you but it is better to be safe than sorry, with the added precaution. There are many agencies online that you can register with.

## Run A Pet Resort/Retreat

Many times when pet owners have to go away for any period of time their big concern is where to leave their beloved animals. If you are fond of animals you can offer a pet resort or retreat service. You can offer a place to house animals for days, weeks or months; the longer term is sometimes known as pet fostering. An example of when fostering may be requested is where the pet owner themselves are the victim in an abusive relationship. They may have chosen to stay in that situation because they were fearful of what could happen to their pet if they were to leave suddenly. Therefore, offering this kind of service can also be great for both of you. Be sure to do your research and inform your insurance company. Take caution when inviting animals into your home as you may find that as they settle in they may be more destructive than you first realised. Therefore take care to remove any valuables from the area of your home that the pets will have access to.

## Pull Money Out of Retirement

Another highly effective way to secure funds for leaving your partner is to delve into your retirement fund. It is time to face the facts; if you are in an abusive relationship and you stay, there is a chance you won't ever be able to even use the retirement money because you could end up dead. The statistics for spousal homicide when abuse is previously reported is very high, so do not take any chances with your life. Getting away from your abuser safely is crucial. On the other hand, securing your safety with the appropriate funding is necessary. Fortunately your nest of retirement funds can provide the funding fast and efficiently, and can be rebuilt at a later time.

Before pulling money out of retirement you need to know that you may end up having to pay a penalty. Penalties are put in place because the money for retirement was set to come out at a certain age. If the age was 59, and you're only 32, you may end up having to pay a 10% penalty on the amount you withdraw. On the other hand, there may be a set fee for withdrawing any amount, or you may simply be required to withdraw a set amount to avoid any fees at all.

Determine how much you want to withdraw, consider the fees, and then make your withdrawal. You'll have to sign paperwork and will often have to wait several business days before the funds are available.

Once the money is available you can then transfer them into your bank account where they can be kept until you are ready to leave your spouse.

## Get a pay day advance

A pay day advance is recommended only if you are unable to obtain a pay cheque early from your boss. Always go for the most affordable and convenient solution first. A pay cheque obtained early often needs little to no paperwork from your place of employment, and it incurs no interest. On the other hand, a pay day advance does incur interest and you end up    paying extra for the advance. While not ideal, these advances can be a lifesaver and are often handed out quite easily to individuals even with bad credit or no credit. Simply bring in a few pay cheque stubs to show how much you make and request an amount from them. This often results in same day payments in cash which is why some prefer this option as opposed to a loan (which often has to go through an approval process if your credit score is not high enough).

Always make sure that you pay back any advance taken out. This is because you can wind up in a world of financial trouble because of the exceedingly high interest rates and fees placed on late payments. There is no sense jumping from out of the frying pan into the fire, so try to exhaust all other sources of funding first before going for a pay day advance.

## Social Lending Sites

Going even one step further, nowadays you no longer have to approach a High Street bank to borrow money or even to save. There are online person to person loan companies; sometimes referred to as peer to peer or p2p loan companies that we can apply to, with everything done via the computer. This will be your last resort. These are sites that put people who need money together with people who have money to loan / invest. It may cost you a bit more than borrowing from loved ones and possibly more than other methods mentioned above. Notwithstanding that, I am trying to make you aware of as many options I know of to help you get out of a dangerous situation. I believe that you are better off knowing that you have options than just relying on say family members for example.

Your interest rate for borrowing will vary depending on your credit history and the amount you would like to borrow. The lender benefits from higher returns by investing their cash through p2p loans rather than the lower rate of returns by leaving their money in a current or savings accounts. However, as a borrower you can sometimes benefit from a lower interest rate than you would get through a High Street bank or building society.

Normally with a p2p loan the higher the loan risk, the higher your interest rate will be. If your credit record is not very good you may still find someone prepared to lend to you money, although, it would be at a higher interest rate. It is advisable to first compare loan offers in their entirety before accepting any loan offer; in other words find the best social lending site for your circumstances.

Keep in mind that this can be a riskier approach to getting a loan than going down the traditional routes. Therefore, like pay day loans think long and hard before committing for it.

## Tips For Keeping Your Finances Paper Trail Hidden

Often times if you get a new credit card, apply for a loan, or pull money out of your retirement, you will have official documents sent to your home in the mail. This can easily clue in your spouse to the fact that you are planning on leaving and cause a great deal of distress for you. To prevent this, make sure that you discuss with the advisor or credit card issuer that you are using the money to leave your spouse and that he/she is abusive. Request that all mail be sent either to a PO Box that you have taken out, or to a trusted family member or friend who is capable of holding them and not speaking to anyone about it.

## Phone Calls

Another thing you need to make sure to do is to request that all communications be made through mail that is sent to a PO Box, a family member or your friend. This way if the bank or advisor has any questions or needs to communicate with you, they won't call your phone where your spouse will potentially overhear or answer.

Alternatively, if you have a second phone that you have ready for when you leave, you can direct them to call that number. Simply make sure that your phone is turned off or is on silent so your spouse is not alerted to your secondary phone.

## Hiding Money

The absolute best and most secure place to hide money is with your bank. Not only will this ensure that every penny is kept accounted for but it also means that there is no one else but you who is able to withdraw it. From keeping a safe box at your bank, to holding the money in an account in your name only, a bank is the best possible way to have your money. Make sure that you are able to withdraw your money out at any time – having a working debit card tested prior to you leaving is a must. If however, you need to keep your money elsewhere you can leave it with a trusted friend and pick it up from theirs on your way to your secure location.

## Your Life is Worth More

No matter what method you use to obtain money, keep in mind that your life is worth the cost. Things may seem turbulent and difficult now, especially when you are scrambling for funds to leave. Be assured that they will get better over time. Once you are able to leave your abuser, resume doing normal types of activities, and begin making a steady income at your job without his/her interference, you can pay off any debt incurred during this time. No matter what you pawn, sell, or get rid of in the process, always bear in mind that you are worth far more and that it is a small price to pay when your life is at stake.

Do not stay longer than is necessary simply because you are avoiding pawning something or selling something. If you are faced with a potentially harmful or deadly situation, you need to get out then. There are always emergency groups available to provide shelter, food, and support to you. Should you leave before any of your funding arrangements are made you can go to one of the local organizations, seek help, and get the support you need until your finances are sorted out.

Always make sure that you and your children are safe. Take all of the necessary precautions and make sure to hide all your documentation and cover your trail before you leave. Again as mentioned in a previous chapter, make sure not to irresponsibly tell many family members and friends because they may end up telling your abuser.

**Key
Principle**

There are many ways for you to obtain the finance

you need to help you bring an end to your

existence as an Intimate Slave and start

your life as a Free Fulfilled Individual.

CHAPTER 11

# HOW FAR

# SHOULD YOU GO AND WHAT IF

# YOU OR YOUR FAMILY OWN THE HOUSE?

*"What should you leave behind? All that it takes!"*

 **Author**

### It's worth your life and happiness

*Following all the threats that he had made against me and my family, I knew that I would no longer be comfortable. I also knew better than to move nearby since I had heard too many tragic stories of victims who had underestimated their abusers and come to harm. Armed with my newly found self-esteem, I decided to think outside the box. My initial thinking was going to try and get a SAT scholarship in USA but my family suggested a wonderful point. I would have a wider base of support in the UK than I would in the USA; this was in the form of my aunt and grandmother. Therefore I decided on studying in the UK.*

*Now there seemed to be another hurdle. This was that I needed his signature on a document showing that as a student I had ties to Trinidad to come back to. So I mentioned to him about needing the signature in order to study but I did not say where. I made sure that I was in a hurry when I presented the document to him so as to deny him the time to go through the document in detail.*

*I made all the necessary arrangements but I did not use my home address or phone number for correspondence. In the middle of it all I had to make arrangements as to how my great grand aunt's house would be cared for. This is because we were staying in it and also were chipping in when it came to her needs. I do recall that the night before I left I mentioned the matter to some people because I knew that possibly I would not see them again. I then left the Caribbean for the UK to begin my quest to heal and bring out a better version of Norva.*

*I felt really sad to leave my ex-husband in the house with my late great-grand aunt but consoled myself with the knowledge that they had an 'okay' relationship. I remember on the day I left, I called to inform him that I wasn't coming back. His response was that he would be out of my family house within the week. Over a decade has passed and my great grand aunt is now deceased. During all this period I have heard many people refer to the house as belonging to my ex-husband. It's difficult to know that he chose to remain there. I have had to come to terms with it, especially now that he has his new family living there. I still pray that my family members who are responsible for that property will do what is necessary for them to keep hold of what legally belongs to them. In my situation, I knew that it was not worth it for me to stay in that toxic, volatile, abusive relationship just for the family house. The more I educated myself the more my life was worth to me.*

*The lesson to bear in mind here is that no matter the gravity of the situation, some big decisions will have to be made. At times it is not wise to listen to your heart instead think logically and be real with yourself. I simply had to trust God to direct my steps and He has done a great job.*

# How Far Should You Go?

Leaving is never easy and you don't want a repeat of the same situation when your partner finds out where you are and begins harassing you and stalking you. Making a new life for yourself is essential, and you may have to go to extreme lengths to do that and get away from your abusive ex.

Leaving the home – If you are simply leaving an emotionally abusive relationship that was fairly short term, then simply leaving the home and finding a new place to stay may be all you need to do. Assess how possessive and potentially violent your ex-partner is first because things may escalate to physical violence and threats when you leave.

Leaving the city – Leaving the state may be too big of a step both financially and emotionally, especially if you have friends and family in the state you currently live in. Putting a few hours distance between you and your ex-partner will be more than enough. It can help to ensure you can get on with your life without ever having to see them again. Additionally, leaving the city is often a good distance if you and your ex are going to co-parent your children – this allows for enough space that you don't have to see the ex on a daily basis but it also makes it feasible for the other partner to see the children on a regular basis with a tiny bit of travel involved.

Leaving the state – Leaving the state is a huge step but is needed in many cases where physical violence occurred and where an ex-partner has a high chance of becoming aggressive, stalking, and harassing after the relationship ends. If you want to put a significant amount of distance between you and your ex-partner, then consider finding a new place in a different state. This is also a great way for you to start a new life, reinvent yourself, and find new friends in a supportive community! Taking a leap across state borders is a great and recommended step!

Leaving the country – Sometimes starting over in a new place is needed. If you've got a very abusive ex-partner, then leaving the country may be the last but necessary resort. An ex that is very persistent, keeps stalking you, and keeps harassing you may never be caught and charged by the police. Getting away from everything that reminds you of your ex and eliminating all chances of your ex appearing at your job or at your local super market can be done easily by leaving the country entirely. You often need a lot of money to do this, however if you have family or friends in other countries, then they can help you and provide you with a place to stay during your transition period.

## What if You Own The Home?

If your name is on the lease, or you own the home and you're attempting to leave your abuser, then you have some serious things to consider. Sometimes if a partner is simply verbally and emotionally abusive, then you can simply kick them out of your home, set up a security system and alert the neighbours/landlord about the situation. This is often enough in most cases, although if there is physical abuse and violence involved, then you need to consider your situation carefully.

No amount of money or physical assets is worth more than your life or your safety, so you need to consider the possibility of ceasing immediate tenancy at the home. If you are unable to leave right away because you have not sold the home, then consider changing the locks immediately, setting up a home security system, and also looking to sell it off right away. The chances of being stalked, harassed, and attacked by your ex-partner are very high if you stay in the same location, so you need to leave your old home behind and look for new residency.

Staying at a friend's house or family member's house that the partner does not know the location of is best until you get a new place to stay and get rid of your old home. Make sure that you document the state of the house when you vacate it and keep in mind that you may have to contact the authorities to ensure someone comes by the house from time to time to make sure no damage is done to it.

It is always best, if you are leaving a very abusive and dangerous situation, to simply start a new life when you leave them – get rid of your old job, your old house, and your old town/city because your life is worth far more and you need to be wary of stalking and harassment that can ensue when you leave your abusive partner!

## Your Past Relationships

Leaving the area that you have called home and the house that has sentimental value will be a little heart wrenching, as I discovered. However, embrace that the world we live in today is a lot closer than it was twenty years ago. With social media, Skype and the mobile/cell phone your old friends can still stay in touch. If you miss seeing your old home Google maps can help you out, if you don't have photos of your own.

When I left Trinidad mobile phones were just being introduced and this was back in the day phones looked like solid blocks. In addition, I remember the times when you say goodbye to loved ones at the airport, not knowing when and if you will ever hear from them again. That is a thing of the past. In fact, on some national flights you can even use your phone while on route. Failing that, your lack of communication is just the flight time journey. My point is this; don't feel too nostalgic and sad about what you are leaving behind. Remember, you have your life and you should be grateful for the modern technology all around you. Your life is worth the effort of starting over.

*When I was younger one of my relatives told us about an incident that they had partly witnessed. One of their neighbours had left her abusive partner and she began to set up herself for her new free life. She had left her television behind so she decided that she would go back quickly one day to collect it. My relative related to us that when they saw her they were surprised. They asked her why she came back to which she said that she was just going to collect her television and go away for good. My relative said that they tried to persuade her not to go in, her ex was at home and the television was not worth her life. She felt confident enough, so she reassured them that they shouldn't worry as she would be in and out of there quickly.*

*They watched her as she went in the house. Within a minute they saw her run out the front door of the house, with her ex in hot pursuit. Two of my relatives scrambled down the steps of their house; they could tell that the situation looked intense. The woman had run around the outside of the house. My relative shared that by the time they got in the yard of their neighbour, to where the couple was, something horrible happen. The man's hands were firmly gripping the neck of the woman as he held her face down in a shallow muddy puddle. They were too late, she was dead. One of my relatives simply asked the murderer, 'what have you done man!' my guess is that the now murderer must have been asking himself the same question.*

Rage can show up at any time and once the tendency is already there I want you to commit to yourself that you will not be the one to unnecessarily put yourself in harm's way. Seek to get away as far as is appropriate for you. Shake off the past and be committed to making steady progress in your life. The first place you go after leaving abuse, will most likely not be your permanent place of abode. The important thing is that you give your life and future a great start by thinking positive and looking forward to your freedom filled life. Yes you will sometimes wonder, 'what am I doing?' or 'can I really survive without him?' Yes you can and yes you will. Keep working on your freedom, it's Time To Go!

Key
Principle

You have to be ready to do whatever it takes and

go as far as it takes for you to keep

yourself free and safe.

CHAPTER 12

# WHAT TO DO AFTER

# YOU'VE LEFT THE ABUSIVE RELATIONSHIP

*"Do your part to keep you safe, it will take some effort but the reward that waits will be well worth it."*

☞ **Author** ☜

**Tales of The Unexpected**

*After leaving that relationship by migrating halfway around the world, I spent time working to rebuild my self esteem, self confidence, my academics and providing the best opportunity possible for my baby daughter.*

*During that time a childhood acquaintance came back into my life. I had met him when we were both 13 years old, while on a summer holiday. Over 11 years had passed since our initial meeting so we had a lot of catching up to do.*

*We became the best of friends in no time, began courting and after 3 years got married.*

*The love we have for each other was very evident for others to see. However, we still had heated debates, unmet expectations, feelings of loneliness at times etc. I came into the relationship with a lot of emotional baggage and that compounded some of our issues.*

*I spent time improving myself and we now have a loving healthy marriage. I noticed the good things that my husband does and how much they outweighed the few issues. I treat him like a king and he treats me like a queen.*

*The lessons of that past toxic marriage now help me to greatly appreciate the friendship, respect, support, and love that I have today. I am mindful of the things I say to my husband and excited about surprising him. I am not dependant on him for my happiness or fulfilment. I give, not expecting in return. But my husband does the same for me, helping out around the house and doing those things that I really appreciate without me having to ask or prompt. He indeed is the man of my dreams.*

*It's been over a decade since my husband and I have been married and we are infinitely more in love today than we were in the earlier days.*

*The marriage has been an inspiration and turning point for me.*

*It was because of my experience that I came up with the concept The Wise Wife™ and I've never looked back.*

*Over the years I have had my share of health issues from miscarriages to cancer and difficult births. I have learnt to appreciate the power of a fulfilling relationship, especially during those dark times. None of us know what tomorrow holds. If someone had told me the journey my life would take, I would have said no way, especially during the abusive relationship, not realising the beautiful life to come.*

Once you've left your abuser, things will not be business as usual. Instead, it takes a great deal of time for both you and your abuser to move on with life. Immediately after leaving and relocating, it is crucial that once it is within your power, you cut off all contact with them. You need to break free of their hold and the best way to do this is to avoid them completely. The only things that should cause you to have to communicate with your ex abuser should be if you have children and to finalise your divorce. You do not have to speak to your ex directly either. Use the appropriate services of a lawyer and child services to establish third party communication. If they are aggressive, harassing, and beginning to stalk you, it is essential that you seek help from your local law enforcement agency to get a restraining order. Additionally, don't be embarrassed to share with trustworthy individuals around you about the situation you were in and to have them as allies and supports should your ex abuser decide to come after you. Staying silent can mean the difference between others recognizing that your ex showing up is a possible threat to your safety and them not knowing what was going on. The latter of course can be to your detriment. There are a myriad of other things you can do to keep safe, avoid contact with your ex abuser, and help ensure that there are no confrontations or dangerous situations.

## Staying Safe Inside Your Home

First things first, you need to make sure that if you're in the same house you and your ex lived in, that you should have all of the locks changed and dead bolts installed. Additionally, even if you are in a new location that your ex supposedly isn't aware of, it is crucial that you also put dead bolts on your doors. Another great way to improve your home security is to get new and secured windows (barred windows may be a bit extreme but could definitely keep you safe!). Once you can afford it you may consider replacing all wooden doors with metal doors, and also install a home security system. A home security system is an amazing and cost effective solution to keeping you safe not only from your abusive ex-partner but also from potential burglaries. Just the fact that one is installed and the stickers displayed on the windows can help deter anyone from attempting to break in!

Another home solution is to have motion activated flood lights installed outside. This will help you stay safe at night when you are coming home, and can also deter a potential stranger from attempting to get into your house when they're illuminated sneaking around outside! You can also get motion activated lights set up inside your house as well. This can help ensure that you're never caught off guard and you can always see who and what is in a room without having to turn on a light!

Lastly, consider installing a camera system on your property. This is a step that may seem drastic for some; nevertheless there is no telling what your ex-partner will do. Many victims who have left abusive relationships have had their property damaged including their vehicles, house, and anything in their yard. Because of the high risk for violence, aggression, and potential stalking/harassment post breakup from an abusive relationship, getting a security camera installed can not only help you see who is at the door before you answer it, and who is potentially outside should you be home but it can also be critical pieces of evidence against your ex-partner. The evidence captured can get them put away in jail and punished legally for any harassment and damage they've done to you and your property!

Some other simple and relevant tips to help keep you safe are to:

- Ensure that any bushes, trees and plants on your property are kept well-trimmed because they can be vital hiding places for a perpetrator and can obscure your vision of the property!
- Put strong locks on all buildings on the property including the garage (lock it from the inside if possible!) and shed.
- Make sure that your power box is kept safe because this can be a huge cause for concern if your home phone line is disconnected and your electricity is shut off due to tampering with your power box!
- Have your neighbours keep an eye out on your house occasionally – alert them that you've left an abusive relationship so they know to call the police should something seem amiss.

## Ensure The Safety of Your Children

If you are a parent, then it's essential you keep your children safe. Should you have a restraining order and full custody of your children, then you need to give a copy of that restraining order to all care providers for your children. This means that the nursery, school principal, and babysitter all need to know that your ex-partner is dangerous, is not allowed to take your children, and that the authorities should be called should he/she arrive.

Additionally, consider taking your children to a new school or nursery entirely. It may cause your children to be very upset and have crying spells, tantrums, or stop talking to you but you need to keep in mind that your children can easily be swayed by your ex-partner to go with them. Should your children be in contact with your ex, and your ex takes them, that can be used against you and they could be in serious danger, especially if your ex was violent.

Your children's safety is a higher priority than their current happiness. Relocating them may be the best option, though you will also need to consider counselling just to make sure that any issues your children may have from the violence, relocation, and parental split can be worked through with a trained professional. You don't want your children emulating the violence and aggression that they saw or noticed when you were in a relationship, nor do you want them to become distant with you because of how you're trying to keep them safe.

# Becoming Untraceable

While most people think that simply leaving your ex and relocating to a new home is enough to ensure no more contact, you'd be surprised to learn just how easy it is for an abusive ex to get back into contact with their victims. Unfortunately most people underestimate how predictable they are, and their common habits can easily lead a harassing or stalking ex right back to their victim. In addition, simple things such as social media accounts and phone numbers also allow an ex-partner a very large window to begin harassing and abusing their victims again!

If your ex was physically or mentally abusive to you and caused you to ultimately leave them, then you need to really consider your life and what changes need to be made. It's absolutely crucial that you avoid contact with your ex at all times, so preventing them from "surprising" you while you're out and about running errands is essential. Here we have some general tips that you should take into consideration when you've left your ex:

- Change your number and make it unlisted

The very first thing you should do when you break up with your abuser and leave them is get a completely new phone and number. Using an old phone that you had with your ex is out of the question because there are so many different types of programs that can be installed on the phone to monitor and relay information that yours could easily have been tampered with. Instead, use a different phone either given to you from an abuse organization that is helping you, or from a new mobile phone provider. Once you get this phone, call your carrier and ensure that your number is completely unlisted! Don't give this number out to many people, only those you truly trust and who will not relay any information to your ex abuser. Keeping all forms of communication cut between you and your ex is essential!

- Get caller ID on your phone immediately

Caller ID can allow you to easily screen your calls and stay anonymous. An ex-partner may get your number or have someone else attempt to call the number hoping to confirm it's yours, so screening your calls will ensure you can refuse to answer if you don't recognize who it is. Don't put any identifying information on your voicemail either – it could help confirm who owns the phone number and lead your ex into harassing you again!

- Change your work or hours

If you're employed somewhere, you need to make sure that your employer is aware of the situation, especially if you have a restraining order on someone. Should there be a receptionist available at your work, ensure that they are there to screen who is coming to see you, and to refuse to answer questions as to if you work there or not so that your ex cannot stalk you.

Additionally, if you cannot change your work location, see if you can change your work hours. An employer will generally be more than willing to accommodate your extenuating circumstances, especially if there are authorities involved (i.e. restraining order). See if you can work from home, if possible, or work a different shift so that your ex-partner is less likely to find out and follow you.

- Change your routes and stores

Most people take the same routes to places which can be easy for an ex to identify. Instead of taking the same way into work every day, or going to the same grocery store near you, consider changing all of your driving and shopping habits entirely. See if there is online grocery shopping so that you can stay safe and have all of your groceries delivered right to your door for a few months. Additionally, take the scenic and long way into work, or consider taking public transport for a while.

Should you have a gym membership, or a membership to any club or organization, consider going either on different days or to a different location entirely! These sorts of habits and situations are how an ex can easily find you and learn where you live, where you work, and begin harassing you!

- Never travel alone

If you have to go to the store, gym, or to work, try to arrange it so that you always travel with someone. Pay to have someone from work carpool with you and come pick you up – it may end up to be far cheaper than you driving in every day, and having the company of someone will keep you safe and ensure you're not isolated and feeling alone.

Additionally, if you have to go anywhere else, see if a friend or family member can go with you and your children. You will need the company of others during your healing process after the split, and also their company can ensure that you're not surprised by your partner when you are out running errands.

- PO Box

Consider getting your mail sent to a PO Box that you purchased from your local post office. A PO Box can ensure that you don't have any mail sent to your direct location like general bills or anything else. It can also ensure that if your ex somehow does learn of your mailing address, that they don't know your physical location and cannot harass you there or get into your personal

- Remove them from your Social Media contacts

Last but not least, as I have mentioned throughout this book the aim of the abuser is to control you. When you seek to sever the hold, the next best thing is for them to stalk you or at a bare minimum to keep tabs on what is going on in your life. Based on what they learn about you, your ex abuser may be so obsessed that he begins to react to things you are sharing about moving on with your life. I believe that it is imperative that you unfriend, unlike, cancel subscription, remove from your contacts etc all online connections with your ex abuser. You should also consider doing the same to his close friends and family members as he may access your profile via their connection. You need to also change your passwords if what you have is known by him or he can easily figure them out, for example, maybe because it means something to him or it's your mother's maiden name.

In recent years I have learnt about two incidences worth mentioning:

*First, an ex partner, who is very vindictive broke into his ex partner's Facebook account and posted a number of 'poo porn' images (pornographic images or videos involving the use of human excrement [poo]). He then posted many of the images on her Facebook fan pages and groups, which is how I saw it. It was totally disgusting but quickly went viral, long before she had the chance to realise. By the time she caught on there were thousands of messages in her inbox, many of which were unkind in nature.*

*The next incident involved a 27 year old accountant named* Camille Mathurasingh[1.] *She lived in London. She met a 25 year old young man in Trinidad, during a three year period that she worked there for PricewaterhouseCoopers. She returned to UK when her stint was over. Camille started to have doubts about the future of her relationship with the Trinidadian and tried to bring it to an end. During that time she met a man in the UK and started going out with him. Her ex saw some photos which she posted on Facebook. It showed her with the new boyfriend. Within a couple weeks her ex flew 4,000 miles from Trinidad to UK so he could confront her about the Facebook pictures. He became so enraged that he stabbed her 20 times at her home, before cutting himself and crashing her car.*

I hope that these two cases highlight to you the importance of breaking off all social media and other connections with your abusive ex, because in his eyes you belong to him.

## Understanding Stalking and What to Do About It

Leaving a relationship from an abuser is difficult but keeping away from them and breaking their hold over you in its entirety is the hardest part. Many abusers resort to stalking and harassment for a number of reasons: to try and convince their victims to come back; to try and punish them for leaving; or to try and regain some sort of control over the situation that they recently lost. Stalking is a horrific experience that sadly is very common after a victim has left the abusive relationship. Understanding stalking and how our modern way of life inadvertently makes it easier for victims to be stalked is paramount. You should also learn about what to do if you're stalked; this is crucial to your physical safety and emotional stability. In addition to what you are reading in this book I encourage you to do some research on stalking and other abuse topics. This will help you to be prepared for the unexpected.

## Methods Stalkers Use

Stalkers use a variety of methods to harass and traumatize their victims and unfortunately technology dramatically increases the ease of which they can access and harass their targets. From sending letters, gifts, and cards to victims, to posting information, spreading rumours, and constantly calling a `mobile/cell phone or work phone, there are a myriad of things that cause extensive amounts of distress to victims including:

- Making fake profiles online to message/harass victim and contacts
- Follow the victim and show up at various locations
- Leave notes or messages at a person's house
- Send constant text messages or calls
- Monitor victim via cameras, GPS, or spyware on computer
- Threaten friends and family members of victim
- Damage property

## How It May Affect You?

Stalking is a horrible experience for someone to go through, and it unfortunately leaves a dramatic impact on the victim both emotionally and in their personal/daily lives. Many victims of stalking lose time at work, become very anxious and fear ridden, have difficulty sleeping, worry excessively, are stressed about social situations, develop PTSD (post-traumatic stress disorder), have flash backs, develop eating disorders, and often end up relocating entirely to escape their stalkers.

## Dealing with a stalker

The first thing to realize is that a stalker will usually continue their harassment of you for several months. They go through a slew of attempts and actions to try and get a reaction from you. Once again I would reiterate, especially in the early stages of your life away from your abuser, it is important that you absolutely NEVER make contact with them or respond to them. They feed off the realization that they're getting to you, so messaging or responding in any way is only going to fuel their stalking and make it last much longer than necessary.

Once you know you are being stalked, you need to immediately get a journal and begin documenting it. This is critical because you may need this for police reports and court cases. Keep a recording device for your phone calls and messages at all times, and also make sure that you keep reports of if/when your stalker contacts your work, family, or friends. Additionally, print off all messages and photos being sent to your phone or online – never respond to them but print them off and save them for evidence!

Now that you have the first bit of evidence, you need to immediately go to the police and make a report. File for a restraining order if you don't already have one, and always report violations of that  restraining order to a police department when you're contacted or harassed even after the order.

Understand that stalking can progress to homicide VERY quickly so you need to take every precaution. Let everyone around you know you are being stalked and ensure that they do not message your stalker and make the situation worse. Every time you have a new incident happen from your stalker, make a police report. Sometimes police departments are reluctant to follow up on stalking cases because they may not 'seem serious' at first but once you are persistent about it , your stalker will be charged and can end up with a felony on his/her report due to the stalking (this means serious jail time and lifelong consequences).

Never message your stalker, never rise to the occasion no matter what they say or what they threaten you with. Take every threat seriously and always report. When you stick to this your stalker and ex-abuser will finally get the message that you are never going to respond to them and that you will always bring in the police – they will eventually back off and leave you alone for good!

# Beginning the Healing Process and Rebuilding Your Life

Once you have left your abuser, you are going to feel very different because the ever present abuse is now a thing of the past. Beginning the healing process is difficult, and you may feel the desire to simply give up the fight to ignore your abuser and go back with them – DO NOT. As said previously, never encourage contact with your abuser and always use an intermediary if you need to allow them to have access with your children. Now it's your time to move on and be happy but doing so can be hard.

*Remember that the healing process will not work if you are in contact with your abuser. Eliminate contact and as much as it is within your power never speak with them again about rekindling the relationship, no matter what lies they tell you!

A truly remorseful abuser will take time out to rehabilitate and get all the help and guidance necessary, they need at least six months to a number of years of intensive support. They would give you your space as an individual because they have acknowledged to their self and others that the way they treated you was totally wrong and endangered you. They most certainly will not continue to justify their behavior and actions of the past. Even then it has been said by experts that it is very difficult for an abuser to change and even more difficult for that change to be lasting. Many times they simply give up one form of abusing and take on another. That is because they find it difficult to relinquish the addictive behavior of power, manipulation and control over another individual; especially their current or former victim.

Here's a three step process to get you back on your feet and moving on with your life after an abusive relationship:

1. Start the healing process

Healing after abuse is hard because there are not only physical wounds you may need to heal but emotional ones as well. Start first by simply feeling a great sense of pride in yourself. It's no easy feat leaving an abusive relationship, and yet you've managed to do so! Next, try treating yourself and indulging in something you enjoy. This can be something simple as listening to your favourite music and having a bubble bath, or even going out to a little weekend retreat with a friend and enjoying a spa day!

Another way to begin healing is to go to support groups and see a counsellor. There are long lasting emotional effects from abuse, and you should accept the help available to you. A support group can be a crucial step in your recovery and it is highly recommended for all survivors of domestic abuse. You can not only hear the stories of how other victims are dealing and moving on with their lives but you'll feel a sense of purpose being able to give advice to those who are trying to leave. You will also be connected to individuals who really understand what you're going through. If you haven't yet, then go join our Secret Facebook group[2] and the No Strikes campaign[3]. It's simple to do and the support along with the camaraderie will help you move on mentally by leaps and bounds. That sense of purpose and connection is a powerful feeling and something that can really be a driving force in your recovery!

A therapist or counsellor can address any anxiety and depression issues you may have – which is highly likely. The comments and horrible verbal abuse you've suffered will echo in your head for quite a while after you've left your abuser – making it difficult to really heal and feel good about yourself. With the help of support groups and therapy, you can finally release those negative thoughts and allow positivity to take their place. That is one of the major reasons why you should leave that abusive environment permanently and as soon as possible; the longer you stay the more long term support you will need.

2.  Regain your confidence

This is a huge step and will be a really empowering thing to do. A victim's confidence and self-worth is often shattered when they leave an abusive relationship – this only makes them vulnerable and easily led into another abusive relationship if they're not careful. Instead of falling into the trap of continuous abuse, you need to regain your confidence by first forgiving yourself.

Now, you may think "forgive myself? Why?! "But when you've left your abuser and you're beginning your new life, self-hating thoughts will come over you. Thoughts like "I let it happen, I let him abuse me all of those years" and "I can't believe I let myself lose my family for him". These thoughts will make you feel horrible but it's absolutely critical to know that the abuse was NOT YOUR FAULT. You were not to blame and you need to forgive yourself for not leaving earlier. It's a natural reaction to want to stay and be with a person you love, so don't feel as if you did anything wrong at all!

Another way to gain back your confidence is to get a phrase or mantra to help you when you're feeling down. A great mantra many people use is "Grant me the strength to accept the things I cannot change", however you can use any phrase you want like these below:

- Every day I am born again
- My faith is bigger than my fears
- I live in the present, I've learnt from the past
- I have the wisdom, strength and Grace of God in me
- When I feel like quitting, I remember exactly why I started
- I am loved by God, I am chosen by God, I am protected by God

Repeating a mantra or having it nearby so you can look at it (like on a phone background screen or tattoo), can give you a sudden burst of strength and help you wade through the doubts and hard times with your head held high.

3.  Finding peace

Finding peace is not going to be easy but it is a process like everything else in life. Understand that you probably experienced months, or even years of abuse, so you need to grant yourself the ability to take equally as much time to heal – if not more! Finding peace is not just about forgiving your abuser, or forgetting the past, it's not letting the past control you anymore. You should forgive your abuser mentally and appreciate that you are a stronger individual because of the fortitude you now have.

Forgiving an individual does not mean that you put yourself back in the same unhealthy environment. That would be like buying a comfortable looking shoe that is one or two sizes too small. What if you wore it once to go out and ended up in excruciating pain? What should you do with the shoe, which of the following should you consider:-

- Should you continue to wear that shoe?
- Should you cut off a piece of your feet so it could fit?
- Should you cut off pieces of the shoe to make space for your toes or heel?
- Should you stop wearing shoes all together?
- Why not accept that this shoe is not for you?

I propose that you do the last option, accept that this shoe is not for you. Now back to your ex abuser and the relationship. You cannot make an unmatched, unhealthy relationship work, nor should you try. Both sides would be negatively affected if you try that. Work on you as an individual becoming whole again. This means you need to rediscover yourself, do the activities you loved to do, and gain new life experiences!

## Rebuilding Your Life

There are a number of different things you can do to help you regain your confidence, love life again and stop being consumed by the anguish of your past. Of course we are all different so there is not a one size fit all approach. However, there are a few essential elements which will be common to many. The following should serve as great help to you as you make the mental transition to true and lasting freedom from your past.

- Get Active

First things first, start doing things you used to love to do. Your abuser probably didn't allow you to do certain activities because it boosted your confidence and that was something they didn't like. If you loved mountain climbing, bowling, painting, or even just singing, get back into it again! You're likely going to need practice to re-hone your skills but you need to go back to the things you love because they are a part of you!

Next, try new things! It's probably been a long while since you've done a new experience, so you need to rediscover life! If money permits you, try seeing a new country or doing something super adventurous like skydiving! You've lived in fear and conquered it by leaving your abuser, so enjoying some real life thrills will be absolutely adrenaline rushing for you. It could actually lead you into new and exciting things and hobbies that really empower you!

- Work On Yourself First

Wait at least six months to a year after your abusive relationship before getting into a new relationship. This allows you to rediscover yourself, your values, and what you are as a person. You need to know yourself fully before getting into a relationship else you risk losing your identity and potentially falling for another abuser again.

If someone expresses a great deal of interest in you, then they should have no problem waiting. Those that are worth your time WILL wait for you and will understand why you need them to wait. Concentrate on casual friendships and yourself before ever getting romantically involved with another person again!

- Be Comfortable Being Alone

Don't go searching for a life partner because when the time is right, the right person will come along. Additionally, you need to be comfortable being alone first before you can be comfortable and healthy with another person. This means that you should accept yourself and being alone, be happy, and enjoy finding yourself by filling your time with great activities and things that fill your life with joy. Friends and family can provide you with company and companionship – don't go looking for love because it will appear when the time is right!

- Be Open to New Love Relationships

You may think you'll never find love again, or that you can never trust another person again but you shouldn't live life in fear of a new abuser. Instead, you can learn from your old experiences and use that as a way to enhance your appreciation for loving, respectful individuals in your future love life. You need to be careful about going into new relationships. When you get into them inevitably your past experiences will play a part. Based on where you are with your personal growth and how you view the past relationship, your thoughts and behaviour will be setting you up. Your relationship can therefore end up being a healthy one or head for complete failure before the relationship has a chance to thrive.

Be open to learning and growing with a willingness to listen to people's views and opinion when they say that they have a feeling that something is not right. Whether or not you married your former abuser without doing much digging and research into him and his family, don't repeat the process. When I married my ex-husband, although we had courted for over three years, I was young, naive and impressionable. Even though some people did try to warn me and I saw some things that made me second guess, I asked for some advice and with the positive review I threw caution to the wind. The second time around I chose to inquire much more earnestly. During our early friendship and throughout our courtship, we both took the time to get to know each other's family and friends. I welcomed words of wisdom; listened attentively while I prayed long and hard during those 3 and a half years. I believe that particularly when you have been in an abusive relationship in the past you become cautious and with good reason. Take as long a time as necessary getting to know someone before committing to a long-term relationship and marriage. There may be a need to go for external help and advice so that you do not take the baggage of the abusive past into the new union.

- Be Comfortable Before Going to the Next Level

Should you get involved with a partner, you cannot punish them for the mistakes of previous partners. Every person carries in with them a certain amount of emotional baggage but you need to make amends with your past so that the abuse you suffered does not ruin your current relationship. You can easily find yourself being aggressive and using suppressed anger as a way to hurt your partner. Try talking with your partner and explaining your past to them so that they understand there may be some residual feelings and know how to deal with the situation should issues arise.

I would suggest that you have the conversation once you are at the start of taking your new relationship to the next level. Do not let your pride or embarrassment stand in the way. In a new healthy relationship your partner should be, loving, understanding and patient with you. If this is not the case do not start making excuses for your new partner but communicate candidly and evaluate whether or not you believe that a happy, healthy, fulfilled life can be possible together. If not I would suggest that you cut your losses right away before the situation deteriorates.

- Have Zero Tolerance to Abuse

People treat you how you let them treat you, so it's crucial that you teach your new partner or potential partner that the very FIRST time they show aggression or abusive behaviour to you, that you're not going to tolerate it. You cannot allow yourself to fall into the same trap you were in previously. You're worth far more. Do not put up with being treated in a disrespectful, undervalued manner. It goes without saying that you should talk to someone like a professional, family or friend about any type of emotional or physical abuse so they could help you get out early before you end up in another dangerous situation.

- Don't Rush Into Marriage

A word of warning, although it is not always the case there are many abusers who cover up their personality disorder or abusive nature while dating. Many of them may try to get you to rush into marriage. Look at your potential partner's family and friends closely. This will, in many cases give you a better indication of their true nature and values.

[1]Read a news article on Camille's the story via the first link below:
http://news.bbc.co.uk/1/hi/england/london/8552740.stm
[2] https://www.facebook.com/groups/MyChoiceMarriage/
[3] http://www.mychoicemarriage.com/no-strikes

It will take time and effort for BOTH you and you

abuser to move on. Help yourself and your loved

ones by bringing to a halt all contact or unnecessary

association with your abuser, including

communication and Social [Media]

CHAPTER 13

# WHAT ABOUT DIVORCE

*"When the prisoner is ready to be released, the key to the gate will be made available."*

☞ **Author** ☜

<u>Please read</u>: I am in no way claiming to be a legal professional. The information I give below is based on my experience and research for the purpose of this book. Most of the content in this chapter originates from information that I have gathered from both the U.S. and U.K. It is therefore super imperative that you seek the advice of a legal professional. Treat this information as a sign post and understand that it is not relevant for all readers of this book. Again, please seek independent legal advice.

# Freedom Road

*My mobile rang so I answered. "Hello Ma'am, this is Scotland Yard" the policeman said in a stern voice. I was frightened as I sat in the house with my daughter. I was sure that my ex husband had found me. "Yes, how can I help?" I replied as I tried to remain calm. "Your baby has been playing with the phone and called the emergency number". I breathed a sigh relief and apologised. He confirmed that everything was all right, urged me to be mindful of my daughter's access to the telephone and hung up.*

*I knew that it was inevitable that since my ex-husband still lived with my great grand aunt in her house, he would one day find out where I was. After almost two years of panic attacks and constantly looking over my shoulder, my ex husband found out which country I was now living in. This was apparently thanks to some digging, courtesy of a curious neighbour in Trinidad. He got in touch via mail, and then called my aunt in the UK to get in contact with me. This establishment of contact by him had a mixed impact on me. I was nervous because he now knew exactly where I lived. On the other hand though, I knew he was in Trinidad (some four thousand miles away) when he called and by the conversation we had, I could tell that he still had financial difficulties, so much so that he was in no particular hurry to buy a plane ticket!*

*I was relieved when he announced that he was due to start divorce proceedings shortly. However, I could tell that even at that time he was trying to control things and was not willing to acknowledge that his abusive actions led me to leave my home and country.*

*Not long after he chose a lawyer we had a conversation and he asked me to contact his lawyer which I did. The lawyer informed me that the process would be completed in 6 months provided I don't mention about the abuse but divorce on the grounds that both of us agreed that this was what we mutually wanted. For the sake of speed, I agreed. Sadly, I was to find out that his lawyer's definition of speed was quite different than mine. I was also told that I would not need to have my own lawyer as there was no contest and divorce was what we both wanted. The case lasted two long, drawn out years and the lawyer had excuses at every turn as to why there was another delay. My ex husband would call me and leave messages saying, "Can you call me back!" and "The lawyer wants to speak to you". It would then be my responsibility to call in, which I did just to keep the process moving forward.*

*The communication between me and my ex, and me and his lawyer were on some occasions amicable and on others more aggressive. There was usually what felt like a manipulative tone and my ex-husband's attitude came across immature at times. I was asked to agree to do what I saw as unreasonable demands, both within the divorce papers and directly by my ex, all of which I declined. One such request was that I agree in the divorce papers that I be responsible for paying for all flights and other expenses so that he could see his daughter. My ex husband was daring and he even asked me to send personal items for him. During one of his 'requesting' sessions, when he wasn't accepting of my "No's!" but laughingly persisting, I said in a serious tone, "Listen do you not understand that we are getting a divorce? I left because of the way you were treating me?" He replied by reducing the amount of items on his request!*

*When he didn't get what he wanted I was bombarded with threatening, angry remarks about what my friends and family allegedly said or did to him and what he will do to them. I patiently endured the lengthy process because I was a safe distance away from him and I was not going to do anything to jeopardise the divorce being completed.*

*By the time the divorce was finalised I was both relieved and mighty glad that I wouldn't have him in my ears any longer. I was happy and free to completely move on with my life. I did not demand anything from him, including finances or material possession. The three suitcases I left Trinidad with were all I needed; I had my child and our freedom - Yippee!*

193

*One of the key lessons that I learnt during this process is that an abuser will try to assert control at every possible opportunity. Throughout the long drawn-out process I had to know my worth, live in integrity as well as value my freedom and happiness. In hindsight however, I should not have just taken my abusive ex-husband's word or that of his lawyer about the options available in the whole divorce process. I ought to have done my own research and sought legal counsel independent of him and his lawyer.*

The thought of obtaining a divorce brings a rush of mixed emotions for an abuse victim. At times you may be excited at the thought of moving on with your life and at other times you may be sad at the thought of not being able to make your marriage work. As you embark on putting that horrible chapter of your life behind, the process of divorce isn't the easiest and can sometimes be downright scary. You are letting go of the months or years which you have invested; the life and possibly children who are a product of that union are being affected.

Some people are torn about whether or not they should get a divorce, even though they know in their heart that they need to sever ties with their unrepentant abuser. Nevertheless, because of the way that divorce is viewed by those around them they are very reluctant to be associated with the word and stigma it carries. As a victim they may be given some additional labels, which may be quite hurtful like failure, divorcee, unwilling and selfish, by people who are supposed to be close to them. In some societies they will be ostracized and probably never contacted by friends or family ever again.

As the victim you may have gotten the abuser to leave the family home or they may have gone on their own accord. On the other hand, you may have had to leave the house and took the children with you; unless a court order prevented you from doing so. If you are in fear of your abuser for any reason and you haven't yet obtained a restraining order then do so as soon as possible. A lawyer will give you advice on that and the possibility of you keeping possession of things like the house and car, and temporary custody of your children. Bear in mind that any protection that you get is for a specified time period of not more than a year but you can request renewal for up to another year. The likelihood is that you and your abuser will not easily agree on matters so it may be up to the court to divide the property.

# The Legal Separation and Divorce Process

## Separation

There are many couples who decide to live apart but not to divorce. As a victim of abuse you will need to choose whether being separated is enough for you initially and for the long term. Equally, you can wait to see what your abuser will do, are they ready to move on with their life after a lengthy period of separation from their victim? I would suggest that you carefully consider your options with a lawyer. While separated, you can have a Deed of Separation drawn up to record any agreement regarding financial matters, children and the possibility of getting a divorce in the future. Some states in the U.S. do not have the option of legal separation procedures for couples.

For religious or other reasons some people may decide to never get divorced. As a victim in the U.K. you can still make the separation final by Judicial Separation; this process is not very common. Judicial Separation is similar to divorce but you cannot remarry, the court can also settle any disputes regarding children and financial disputes with the exception of pension splitting.

## Temporary Hearing

A divorce trial could take some time before it starts, on average a year or so. In the mean time you can have a 'temporary hearing' (also known as a **motion**) to set up temporary child or spousal support and any other important issues. Some of the general reasons that may cause you to seek a motion include:

- A request for temporary child support or custody  arrangement of children

- A request by one party for continued occupancy of the marital home

- A request by one party for continued but exclusive use of a motor vehicle

- A request for an order/injunction to insure that a health care insurance plan is not cancelled

- A request for alimony or spousal support

- A request for an award of attorney's fees by one spouse

- A request for an order/injunction to insure that neither of the parties can access a joint earned profit or investment account until it is addressed in the divorce court

If you want to start divorce proceedings you have to be able to show the court that the marriage has irretrievably broken down, many times known as "irreconcilable differences" or "incompatibility". The application to the court is called a Petition or Original Petition. The person who initially files the divorce papers is known as the "petitioner" by the courts and the other person in the divorce is known as the "respondent" or, in some states in the U.S. the "defendant." The petition, which is a letter of complaint, can, at the same time, be accompanied by a request for restraining order, protective order or temporary orders pertaining to child support and alimony. Filing the petition should be based on one of the following grounds:

- **Unreasonable behaviour U.K. or Cruelty U.S.**

As a victim this may be one of the options you choose because many different forms of abuse fall under this category. Your partner's behaviour or indiscretions has led you to not be comfortable to live with them anymore. This covers all sorts of bad behaviour. Consider the reasons and summarise it in a few short paragraphs of your petition (the application for divorce). You should try not to be spiteful or too emotional as it can negatively affect your negotiation and case on the whole. Fresh evidence is important. You should file within six months of you finding out or of an incident taking place. Equally, you could have been living apart from within six months of that period and can corroborate your statements.

- **Desertion U.K. or Abandonment U.S.**

Your spouse has willfully deserted you for over two years without your agreement and without good reason.

- **Adultery**

Your husband or wife has committed adultery and you find it unbearable to live with him or her. You should file this within six months of you finding out or have been living apart from with that period of finding out about the adultery.

- **Irreconcilable differences U.S.**

It is commonly known as a no-fault divorce. No misconduct in the marriage needs to be filed for a divorce. However, the decision and agreement to end the marriage is necessary.

- **Separation U.S.**

In each state there is a specific prerequisite of time period for separation. This can range from six months to three years. The couple must demonstrate that they have not had a physical relationship during that separation period, as the period may need to be restarted.

- **Two years' separation U.K.**

You have lived separately for longer than two years and your spouse consents to the divorce. This is also known as a 'no-fault' divorce. If you tried to rekindle the relationship by living together for periods during, that must not add up to more than six months and you must have been apart for least two years altogether.

- **Five years' separation U.K.**

You have lived separately for longer than five years. Your spouse does not need to agree to this. They cannot defend your Petition to the court but they can ask the court to not allow you to have the final decree for the divorce because of a major hardship such as finances.

## A Note About Children.

If there is a child or children involved that are under 16 and those over 16 who are in full-time education. A Statement of Arrangements about each child has to be filed as well.

All these documents have to be in a particular format and have to state specific things. In many circumstances if not all, the petition and your original marriage certificate will both be of necessity. In addition the Statement of Arrangements and other documents that your lawyer will inform you about, then have to be sent via post to your spouse.

Be prepared that the judge may have questions and queries about the information he or she receives in any or all of the documents sent from either you or your spouse. This is especially the case when there is conflicting information being given. It will affect how long it takes for the entire process to be completed. In the U.S. this is called the divorce discovery.

## Using divorce mediation

In the U.S. divorce mediation is a part of the process of divorce whereas in the U.K. it is a recommended option. However, the practice is still not widely known or used in some states or societies. Mediation is method of resolving disputes which should be cheaper and less intrusive than the courts. It involves an independent and impartial third party or parties, the mediator/s, who helps both come to a mutual agreement. The broad use of mediation includes family, community and commercial dispute resolution. Divorce mediation process is a type of Family Dispute Resolution (FDR). For divorcing couples, where abuse is not a part of the reason for the breakdown, I believe mediation is a viable option for both parties to negotiate a settlement between each other; in some cases with their lawyer present.

The mediation process may not go into the same depth of financial disclosure as the court but for mediation to work the clients need to provide that information to the other mediating party. When one person does not provide relevant information, or has worries about being in the same room as a former partner, or there is an imbalance of power the mediation case can break down. Therefore, in cases where it was an abusive marriage there needs to be better screening and understanding by the authorities. In the past some victims and advocates had felt that there was a lack of impartiality at times of screening; especially when the initial session with both parties was a joint meeting.

Another point was that some mediators were not able to control things, when there were high levels of conflict.

A cunning abuser can attempt to use the mediation process to their advantage, by the use of a range of well orchestrated strategies. Pretending to be emotionally hurt, sensitive to the victim's feelings or frustrated by not being heard, are common scenarios that have been successfully used to get their way. The abuser will try crying and taking some responsibility to get others on their side.

Particularly in the U.S. if mediation doesn't resolve the issues a trial date will be set. Both the victim and the abuser will have the chance to argue their cases before a judge. Safety measures can be put in place to ensure that you are free and comfortable to give your testimony. Discuss before hand, with your attorney, what will be expected of you during the case, how to phrase things and the behaviour that is appropriate. The judge will then examine all the evidence and make a decision for the divorce settlement.

However, clients need to understand how mediation works before deciding if it is the right option for them, and not just be swayed by the cost effective element.

## Using Do-It-Yourself Divorce

If you choose to get divorce on the grounds of Unreasonable behaviors (U.K.) or Cruelty (U.S.) or include it in your application, you must fill in the appropriate form and list all of the facts, not just the results of the abuse. In some states in the U.S. and other countries around the world you may be able to do it yourself. However, if you are not familiar with divorce law and you are clueless as to what you should expect during the process then get assistance. Think about the effect the entire situation is having on your physical and emotional health and ask yourself if you need or want to add that extra stress of working through complex documents. In addition, if you are representing yourself it will be your responsibility to get copies of the orders issued to the relevant individuals.

## Using Online Divorce

Sometimes when a decision is made to terminate an abusive marriage, you may feel the urge to choose the quickest and easiest way to distance yourself from your abuser. However, I would suggest that no matter how you feel, don't go for what seems easiest in your head. Think logically and conduct a bit of research. You can check out statistics and stories via your local library, printed and online information, where your searches can't be traced.

There has been a recent surge in the number of companies offering online divorce, particularly because it is much cheaper than using a lawyer. Bear in mind that online divorce providers do understand the divorce process, they know how to prepare for filing the necessary documents and they can factually answer your questions. Notwithstanding that, they are normally not lawyers and therefore cannot provide legal advice or negotiate a settlement with your spouse. In addition, they cannot advise you on whether or not an agreement that the two of you have reached is fair or is in your best interest. The crucial point for you to consider about online divorce is that both parties must consent and agree to the divorce, have no dispute over assets and totally agree on the child care arrangement.

Contrary to popular belief the length of a marriage is not at all regarded when enquiring about an online divorce. Once you meet the above criteria only then will I say to consider this quick and more economical option to end your abusive marriage. Most abusive relationships will have too many disagreements for this method to be used.

## Be prepared for the lies

The fact that you are seeking to end all forms of your abuser's control over your life may cause them to try any last ditch effort possible to sabotage your life. They may build up hatred for you. Because they know you fairly well, they will try to hurt where they believe you will feel it most. For example they may try to get charges made against you, emotionally blackmail you and bombard you with letters, calls, texts or images; all to see how they can psychologically destroy you.

It is important that you keep in mind that were being abused by your spouse because they want to control and manipulate you. The fact that you are now trying to distance yourself from them completely or even if they are the one who initiated divorce proceedings does not stop them from trying to continue their reign of power and control over you. As a victim, if you are not prepared, you may be blindsided and amazed by both the level of deception and trickery on show throughout you divorce procedure and so doing, many people will believe them and be willing to question your character and integrity. Some abusers start the campaign to be portrayed as the victim long before the divorce process starts. Once they have caught wind that you are possibly thinking of ending the marriage they may seek to be vindictive and do all that is in their power to have you arrested for the most trivial things. Whereas, you were willing to put up with the abuse for years I have heard of how abusers have had their victims locked up for pushing them, throwing an item at them etc. You must try not to retaliate, no matter what and how your spouse tries to get you. If you are charged this could greatly affect your divorce and custody case, not to mention the possibility of you not being able to go back into your family home. If you are locked up, what you have in your possession when you are arrested by the police may be all that you have to start your life over. In addition, until the court says it is ok for you to see your children you may be denied access to them for some time.

As your abuser focuses on being deceptively pleasant and convincing during the trial, you must be prepared and focus on presenting all that the court requires in the manner that it is requested. Keep your emotions in check, be as professional as possible and let the legal system work for you. Always keep in mind that your aim for seeking to obtain the divorce is to sever all ties with the manipulator as quickly as possible.

Your abuser is well versed in their craft and may be secretly upgrading their skills for their divorce show. Do not be surprised by them acknowledging that they have done you wrong but that they are not the only one; you did your part as well. Your abuser may speak about how much they are suffering in different areas of their life because of the hurt and pain caused by this entire ordeal. They describe in detail their part as a downplayed version of the events and embellish your contribution; this will help them gain more sympathy from untrained and unsuspecting members of your families, the legal system and others. For example an abuser may speak about how they pushed or grabbed you, but that was after you took a long time winding them up or saying hurtful uncalled for remarks that were lies. Expect to hear about how they possibly snapped after holding it together for as long as they could.

Another strategy that is commonly used by them in the presence of others is to share that they have now changed since getting help and support for their part in the breakdown of the relationship. They may share about their hope and prayer that you are able to get the help you need so that you can both move on from the bitterness and resentment that as evidently built up in you. They may emphasize that they are not trying to say unkind or spiteful things about you; they are simply making an observation. However, with that may also come their secret attempts to intimidate and terrorize you with threats to harm you, your children, other family members or your pets.

Once an abuser feels like their strategies and tactics are working they will continue to pursue it for as long as it serves them. They may continue to use the courts and other public media to pester the victim for years. Therefore, you should think long and hard about what you seek to get from them through the courts, how much contact with them will you have to endure? Consider the effect that your interaction with the abuser has on you, whether in person or over the phone depending on the level of danger perceived. It is sometimes hard to tell but many times the abuser may have a fear of abandonment, consequently they use any means necessary to stay in any type of relationship with you.

## The Narcissist During Divorce

If you believe that your former abuser has narcissistic tendencies or any other such behaviour disorder, be sure to mention this to your lawyer. This will help them to better prepare for what to expect from the abuser and they can also disseminate the information to other appropriate individuals. Even before the divorce proceedings start, it is important that you work on rebuilding your self-esteem; it will not be a quick fix, so you need to continue even after the divorce is over. Lean on friends and family for support but make sure you get professional help to return to your best self and beyond. In all your interactions with a narcissist you should all be ready for their drama and keep the sessions as mellow toned as possible. You must keep your composure intact so that you don't feed their appetite for attention. Ask to be excused when you feel yourself wanting to explode. Hug someone or cry in private if you have to, then relax as much as possible before returning in the room.

## Custody Caution

For those that are parents, do not be surprised at your abuser's efforts to have joint custody or increase access to your children. Their motive can either be genuine, a maneuver to have more interaction with you, or both. This can prove to be one of the most confusing and stressful part of the divorce. Particularly for mothers, you can be torn between wanting your children to have their father as a part of their lives, and being fearful of the compromising position you will be putting them in, especially if they will have private time with him.

You may be ridiculed for your hesitation at allowing your abusive spouse contact with your children. From the victim's perspective it is likely to come as a surprise that legal authorities, at times inadvertently, send out mixed signals: you should not keep your child in the abusive environment and yet when you are out you should give that same abuser unrestricted access to the children. Don't act maliciously about the issue of access but if you do not feel at ease about any one of the following issues: your abuser's violent nature, sexually inappropriate nature, or the sadistic conversation they may have around your children; do keep reiterating these during the legal process. Furthermore, ensure that you make documentation on every occasion that you articulate to the authorities about these serious reservations. Speak out loud and clear about not wanting to allow your abuser unsupervised access to your children. There are too many tragic stories of abusers hurting or killing their children for selfish reasons, for victims not to be cautious.

## Get support and advice

As I have said in previous chapters make sure you gather as much evidence as possible, include secretly recorded and documented conversation, additionally if you get credible witnesses, who can testify on your behalf that will be a bonus. Your abuser's tactics may make you feel guilty, and have you question your worth, you may see yourself as a failure so throughout this process and beyond you should ensure that you don't go at it alone. Get emotional support from both men and women, as they may be able to help you remain in balance as they share with you from their perspective. There are a large number of nonprofit organizations, government agencies and private practices that provide services for individuals in abusive relationships. There may be a fee for these services.

## Changes in relationships

*A friend of mine, who I had known since I attended primary school, recently shared with me about the change she had noticed in my attitude when I was with my ex-husband. She told me that I was very short in my conversations and that I looked very annoyed, especially when she met me in his presence. I acknowledged that she was right. At the time I didn't realize that I had changed, I remember hoping that I won't be asked any questions about life in general. She shared how refreshing it was to speak to me a few years ago, she phrased it, 'I spoke to the Norva I remembered from school days'. We now have a much better relationship than we ever did.*

Do not feel like you have to defend yourself or persuade anyone; be as loving as you can without stressing yourself further.

It may mean that you have to limit or cut the interaction with some individuals, particularly if you feel that because of the relationship that they have with both you and your spouse, it compromises your safety. Have a conversation with them if you can and explain the reason for your actions. Hopefully in time, they will better understand why you had to do that. Acknowledge and accept your sadness, have a good cry if necessary but take your time and move on from it.

There will be some individuals who will draw even closer to you at this time. Embrace their understanding, support and any help given, even if you believe you don't need it. This is not the time to shut down or get cut off from society. This is a mentally exhausting period for you and others. In some cases it will take a few years before you can revisit some friendships, as you both continue to grow, understand and accept it for what it is.

Some friends will genuinely not know what to say; give them their space and allow them to work through the difficult information. On the other hand, for those friends who seem to be too judgmental or invasive, let them know that you are not happy with the discussion.

## Dealing with Your Anger

From the time you begin to face the reality the life you are living is detrimental to you, be it mentally or physically, you will begin to get angry about where you are and what you have accepted. A little anger is a good thing, as it helps us become uncomfortable with injustice. But sometimes we get stuck in that anger and that is not good for you. The trick to not getting stuck is to not dwell on the place you were but focus on where you are going; your visions, your dreams, the not again reality, I am free etc. Recognize this feeling of, 'How dare you treat me like that and how silly was I to take it?' Acknowledge your part in the intimate slavery you found yourself in; whether it was your action or inaction that had an impact. Whatever the reason, you did not deserve to be treated the way you were. Rejoice in the fact that you are taking the steps to be totally free, that you have the support of loved ones, whether blood relative or not.

Now, you must forgive yourself. Yes, forgive your errors in judgment, your naive character, your wanting your abuser to die and anything else that comes up. Forgiving yourself is the initial step to your freedom. Make sure you truly do it. Then forgive your ex, so that you can set yourself free. This is not 'the forgive and forget' method. No, this is forgiving to take the weight off your shoulders, the stress of failure. You are now given the gift of a stress free existence detached from ever having the impact of that abuse ever again.

If you decide to never release the anger and resentment it will impact your health, your children, and loved ones. Research done at the Ohio State University looked at how people could control their anger. The study found that the effect of anger was the same whether expressed openly or internalized. Anger contributes to illnesses such as high blood pressure, Irritable Bowel Syndrome (IBS), cardiovascular issues, etc. You have to get it out of your head; get professional support, lean on your support network and possibly start journaling if you don't.

When divorcing, spouses are driven by anger. They in turn rack up a great lawyer bill as they may need to retain their lawyers for longer periods to fight their battles. Take a time out to process anger and accept it as part of releasing the past, but don't expect the feeling of being free to happen overnight, it takes time and effort.

## The Clean Break Divorce

In June 2014 the House of Lords in the U.K. received its second reading in Divorce bill (Financial Provisions) to limit the maintenance payments to three years, by making changes to the Matrimonial Causes Act 1973. At present there is no such cap in place and in some countries and states the Judges are free to make Joint Lives Maintenance Orders under which one ex-spouse must make periodical payments to the other for the rest of their lives.

The Bill, which was introduced by Baroness Deech, who feels that the law is outdated in the sense that it is still attempting to put women in the position they would have been in, had the marriage not ended. She believes that the primary aim of maintenance should be rehabilitative as opposed to permanency.

Sometimes in the relationship, one spouse - for whatever reason -agrees not to work, and maybe gives up their career for the sake of their family. But that spouse should not be punished for a collective decision. Equally the working spouse should not be made to pay indefinitely. Both the U.K. and U.S. are now taking a similar approach to moving away from what is called joint life maintenance in the U.K. and permanent alimony in the U.S. The principle behind the proposals is to shift towards a more pragmatic, sensible and fair viewpoint on maintenance.

## Final words on divorce

A word of warning about the information you give to the courts - whether in person or on paper, use as much detail as possible to describe what happened in your toxic relationship. However, do not use undiagnosed terms to describe your spouse, for example pathological liar, psychopath, sex offender, schizophrenic etc; as it will discredit your testimony. You should leave making a diagnosis to qualified experts.

If either the court decides that you are not entitled to get any compensation, or your ex-spouse refuses to pay even though they were ordered to, or you do not want anything from them, don't let it overwhelm you. Go back to school if necessary, or at least get some training and do what is necessary for you to be independent as soon as possible. If you should research people like the singer Tina Turner, author J.K. Rowling, actress Robin Givens and actress, writer and comedian Brett Butler you would see that they have all had illustrious careers after divorce, and three of them after escaping an abusive marriage. You can have a great life, work towards it and have faith; it will keep you strong on those not so rosy days.

At the end of the divorce and once it has been granted move on with your life. There may be things that you still need to do through the legal system, continue with that. You may have been living in fear for years, so to now be free; you will feel a little strange at first. Pat yourself on the back and have a little celebration because you have 'Overcome through Change™.' Now you must continue to grow as an individual and Stand in your greatness. Be confident, be wise and don't succumb to any tactic of your ex or any other individual of a similar character. I have heard of how easy it is for a person to keep falling in love with individuals who are of a similar nature to their ex-spouse. You must guard yourself from going back into another abusive environment.

Key
Principle

The last steps to being totally and legally

free from your abuser are not always

straightforward and can be mentally

exhausting but it is well worth it.

CHAPTER 14

# THINGS TO REMEMBER

*"Your abuser uses control over you the victim. In essence he / she is a Con [artist] Trolling over the perimeter of your life."*

☞ **Author** ☜

Abuse in all its forms is a crime, we need to get away from the environment as safely and quickly as possible because if done on a whim we risk having more harm done than good. Your abuser is a control freak! In other words he is 'a *Con [artist] Trolling over your life.*' You have all the power to break free.

Preparing to leave your abusive spouse. No one, no matter what the circumstances, deserves to be mentally, physically, or emotionally abused. Everyone deserves to be treated with dignity and respect;

regrettably sometimes people get into situations where they are treated otherwise. No one wants to be the victim in an abusive relationship but when a person becomes the victim, it is absolutely imperative they leave as soon as they safely can. Abusers come in many different shapes and forms. Once an abuser feels as if they have the power over their spouse or significant other, they will do everything in their power to ensure the relationship continues that way. They enjoy the power and feeling of superiority, so they often employ a myriad of manipulation techniques to keep their victim with them. From destroying self-esteem, to emotional blackmail, their victims are often subjected to horrible and unfair treatment.

- Make a decision, seek help, take action

- A relationship can easily turn deadly when it is being ended. The lack of control can make an abuser freak out and become far more aggressive and unpredictable than before. This means that you need to be extra careful and extra cautious when leaving.

- Never underestimate your abuser and never accept their sob story when leaving because they will do anything and everything to get you back. Sever all social media ties and other connections that will encourage your abuser to stalk you.

- There are organizations out there to help you, so if you need to leave just in a single day and you've not made enough plans, don't worry. You can be rehoused in an emergency housing or you can even go to a shelter for battered women. If you have children, you need to make sure social services understand the situation and they can either put the children with a family member, or place them in a temporary foster home just until you are in a safe location where you can have them again!

-   Your safety is of paramount importance. Nothing is more vital than your own safety and that of your children. Do not worry so much about physical possessions if you don't have the time to, always make sure that you have an escape plan if you need to leave at a moment's notice!

-   A restraining order can be put in place to keep you safe. This means that if you go in and file for a restraining order, you have documented proof of your fear of your partner. Additionally, you have a reason for your partner never to come around and harass or stalk you. If they do, you can contact the police and report them for violation of the restraining order – this will help significantly reduce chances of you being stalked after you break it off with them!

-   Don't act differently on the day of your planned departure. Your partner can be put on high alert and you can easily tip them off by acting differently or by leaving bits of information around the house.

-   Don't make your plan widely know, be very discreet with it and don't tell too many people you're leaving. Do not feel obligated to tell loved ones especially if they have a good relationship with your abuser. Under no circumstances should you let slip to your physical abuser that you are planning to leave him.

-   Don't ignore threats from your ex-partner even if you've never been physically harmed before. Keep in mind that they will be irrational and can actually make good on those threats, so record EVERY phone call and message for evidence in the courts. This is not a person you love, this is a person who has hurt you and you are no longer responsible for their life. They need to be held accountable for their actions and if you don't follow through with the correct procedures for pressing charges, alerting the police, and taking them to court, it can allow their actions to escalate and turn potentially deadly as a response!

- Whether it is in the abuser's nature or it is a learnt behaviour you should not remain the object of their destructive behaviour. Equally, you must keep in mind that you cannot fix or heal your abuser. He gets a trill from controlling you and keeping you in intimate slavery. He does not care about your feelings but to appease you he may allow the occasional indulgence.

- Don't remain in the relationship because you feel financially trapped. There are a number of ways for you to get extra money so that you can finally leave your abuser and start a new life. Make a list of names of individuals that you can ask for assistance and a list of institutions that you can approach for a loan, then go out there and try. In addition see if you have personal possessions that you can sell to raise the cash you need.

- You need to think long and hard about where you go after leaving abuse to start your new life. How far you go should be dependent on the level of control and abuse that you believe your abuse is capable of and how easily you believe it will be for them to let you get on with your life. It may be that you have to say goodbye to a life and community that you have called home for years. However, your future holds a myriad of opportunities that you can look forward to.

- The longer you remain in the abuse the more damaging affect it has on you mentally, physically and indirectly on your health. With that in mind you need to understand that the time to leave is now. After you leave you will need support to help you thrive and the great women that you are.

- Most importantly try and never dwell negatively on your horrendous and ghastly past. Keep in mind and focus only on the gleeful and auspicious future that lies ahead of you.

- The process of divorce can be mentally and physically draining on you as a person. You must rely on the support of loved ones during this time. No matter how much your abuser tries to ignite your anger, try to remain calm and be as professional as possible throughout the case. Say to yourself, I am too close to my freedom to let you get any satisfaction from my retaliation.

I pray that this book gives you the knowledge and tools you need to help you make the decision which is in your best interest that is to leave your abuser.

Do not say, 'if he does it again I will leave him', because the next time you could end up mentally damaged, mentally ill, physically hurt, severely damaged, permanently damage, comatose or dead. You deserve a happy fulfilled healthy life, in a healthy abuse free environment and you can have it. Success waits for you, so join me by agreeing to work on setting yourself free of this abusive miserable existence where you are not a wife but enslaved. Be a victim no more, it's Time To Go!

Key
Principle

Most victims don't remain in abuse for justifiable

reasons but because they have believed the

lies said to them without examining the

facts and opportunities around them

# METHODS OF ABUSE

*"When you see the abusive signs please don't ignore them and wait for the symptoms."*

☞ **Author** ☜

This chapter is dedicated to highlighting the number of ways that a victim can be abused. Some methods were discussed in previous chapters of this book. However, many of them go unnoticed for what they are, methods of abuse and abusive language. The methods have been divided into categories. Some of them are repeated under different categories because there is a degree of overlap. I hope that by going through this list, which is by no way exhaustive, you will become more aware of the language that you and others may be using, even if done inadvertently.

# Terrorize and Intimidate

Publicly and privately scare a victim by extreme predictable or unpredictable, unreasonable warnings or reactions.

Threats (Deliberate, inappropriate warnings of how they can and may harm. They threaten security or safety and violate others' personal boundaries)

- Victim
    - o  Stop you from leaving them
    - o  Physical harm
    - o  Emotional harm
- Your children
    - o  By taking away
    - o  Physical harm
    - o  Emotional manipulation
- Pets
    - o  By taking away
    - o  Physical harm
- Others the victim cares about
- Commit suicide

May use - Intense and unprovoked aggression; it can be in a vocal tone or by action.

### Verbal Threats

Yelling and screaming

- The victim
- Children
- Others the victim care about

- Pets

Cursing

- The victim
- Children
- Others the victim cares about

Criticize

Punishing or ridiculing

Excessive punishment or ridiculing

- Children
- Pets

Addressing with harsh words

- The victim
- Children
- Others the victim cares about
- Pets

Physically Harm

- The victim
- Children
- Others the victim cares about
- Pets

Abandonment (e.g. leave stranded)

- The victim
- Children
- Others the victim cares about
- Pets

## Kill

- The victim
- Children
- Others the victim cares about
- Pets

Make victim witness them harm:

- Children
- The victim's loved ones
- Pets
- Others

NB: May be done in person or via video

Make victim hear them harm others or animals:

- Front close proximity
- On phone
- Recorded

Give details of a malicious act the abuser has done:

- That's the truth
- That's a lie

Excessive teasing

- To the victim
- Others

Hostility towards the victim:

- Among family members
- Among Others

Demands (Inconsistent or unreasonable requests)

- E.g. get the victim to get out of bed, stay in one spot, eat poo (yes it does happen) etc

Betrayal Threats

- E.g. To reveal personal or embarrassing information
  - o To the victim only
  - o In the presence of others

Invalidation (the victim is made to believe that as a person, their beliefs and values are substandard or worthless)

- E.g. saying their belief is a load of crap, what you just said was rubbish, you are so stupid etc.
  - o To the victim only
  - o In the presence of others
  - o Circular Conversations (Almost unending arguments or constant repetition of what has been said with no resolution)

Destroying possessions

- The victim
- Children
- Others the victim cares about

# Constant Monitoring or 'Checking Up'

Thought Policing (interrogation to control your thoughts or feelings)

Online monitoring

- of the individual via their postings to friends

- of the individual in their communities (group and forum)

Mobile/cell phones

- Tracking your location (known or unbeknownst to you)
- Excessive phoning
- Read-through (known or unbeknownst to you inspection )
- Excessive texting

# Control or Coercion

Instructing - Excessive and unnecessary

- Where you can and can't go
- What you can and can't do
- What you can and can't say
- What you can and can't wear

Accusations  (unwarranted or exaggerated criticism)

Condescending (deliberately and maliciously talking down at or about you, consciously lower yourself from a superior position)

- E.g. To tell a victim I don't blame you for not knowing a simple thing like that', you're a woman.

Harassment  (continuous pattern of unwelcome behaviour) towards:

- The victim
- Their loved ones
- Their colleagues
- Others that are in some way connected with the victim

Ranking and Comparing

Compulsive Lying (lies all of the time or more often than tells the truth, out of habit)

- Without regard for the consequences to others
- Without having an obvious motive to do so

Projection (Attributing one's own feelings or traits to another person)

- Fantasize that the other person has those same feelings or traits
- Believing that the other person has those same feelings or traits

Unfounded Blame (Identifying a person as responsible for creating a problem)

Use of undue pressure to:

- Make or change an advance health care directive
- Give money or other possessions
- Female circumcision
- Move out of the home

# Humiliate or Insult

Scapegoating (Singling out for unmerited negative treatment or blame)

Targeted Humour

- Mocking
- Sarcasm
- belittle

Intentional embarrassment done publicly

- In the victim's presence
- Without the victim's knowledge
- With the victims' knowledge, and not in their presence

Betray confidence with sensitive information

Start rumours

Scared in the presence of others

- Threaten to betray confidence
- Threaten to start rumours

Belittling

- E.g. Told you are not good enough

Shaming (Cause someone to feel inadequate or that they are appalling)

Taunt

- With or without a friendly twist
- To the victim only
- In the presence of others
- Directly
- Indirectly

Ill-speaking

- To the victim only
- In the presence of others
- Directly
- Indirectly

Degradation (to lower in dignity or estimation; bring into contempt)

Demeaning (because you don't consent, e.g. to sexual activity)

Teasing and ridiculing (Excessive and unprovoked poking of fun)

- About mental capabilities
- About physical appearance

Labelling or name-calling (powerful negative stigma placed on a victim that affects their self-concept and social identity)

- E.g. Sweaty, dog face, fatty, lazy, ugly, stupid, know-it-all, Jesus-freak etc.
    - o   With or without a friendly twist
    - o   To the victim only
    - o   In the presence of others

Patronizing (Belittle by pretending to respect the victim when they don't' because they know more in some way)

- E.g. tell a victim I love to hear what you have to say, then ignore or disregard what they say.

Comparing you to others (to belittle you or your loved ones)

May use - Profane, derogatory or dehumanizing terminology to describe you or your loved ones

# Ignore or Rejection

Disparaging

- Remark
- Action

Order to leave

Refusing

- To speak to
- Physically touch

Refusing to give

- Love

- Communication
- Attention
- Touch

Abandonment

- Physical
- Emotional

Kicking out of the home

Locking a victim out to discipline or punish

- The home
- Vehicle
- Building
- Event

Wilfully or instinctively let a victim feel unwanted

- E.g. rudely comment to a victim that you don't know why they are present

Snub or shunning (insult by pretending to not even notice)

- E.g. The victim from their family or friends altogether

Slight (treat without due respect or as unimportant)

- E.g. Pay no attention to the victim, while acknowledging everyone else in the room

Scorn (show dislike, open contempt or disdain; the victim is made to feel they are not worthy of any respect or approval)

- E.g. What is that doing here?

Putting down (say no to a request without just cause)

- E.g. telling or referring to a victim as having nothing good to offer

Silent Treatment (Displeasure, contempt and disapproval is shown through nonverbal gestures while remaining quiet)

- To the victim only
- In the presence of others

Withholding or denying

- Affection
- Physical assistance
- Social needs support
- Emotional support
- Medical or health care
- Safe environment

Fail to acknowledge the victim's:

- Presence
- Contribution
- Interests
- Activities

Decline victim's invitation to connect; without just causes by:

- No response
- Harsh response
- Insulting response

Emotional abandonment

- E.g. Refusing to acknowledge your true relationship

# Isolate

Seclusion from seeing or talking with others

Deny engagement

- With You
- With others

Deny association

- With You
- With others
- Institutions

Deny access (the victim)

- To the abuser
- With others
- To basic items

Restricting

- Engagement
- Access to necessities
- Eating

Punishment

- Physical
- Withholding necessities
- Embarrassing
- Insults

Commanding (Have the victim to not do or stop doing what the individual enjoys or wants to do)

- Break off friendships
- Stop social activities
- Decline invitations

# Corrupt

Give or encourage a victim to do or standby and watch immoral activities or disempowering take actions etc. like:

Drugs alcohol and other addictive or illegal substances

- giving to a victim to
  - consume
  - transport
  - sell
- using in the presence

Watch cruel behaviour toward animals

Watch or look at inappropriate sexual content

Criminal activities

- Participate
- Witness

Encouraging harmful behaviour

- To self
- To others

Encouraging, promoting or rewarding unethical or illegal behaviour like:

- Drugs
- Stealing
- Cheating

- Lying
- Bullying
- Promiscuity
- Drug mule (transports drugs across international borders)
    o Knowingly
    o Unknowingly

Encourage to engage in behaviour that is harmful or unhealthy

- The victim
- Others
- Pets
- E.g. Bulimia, Anorexia or unwanted abortions

## Manipulate and Exploit

Hysteria (over-reaction to bad news or disappointments to gain attention)

Pathological Lying (habitually lies to serve their own needs)

Gaslighting (based on the 1944 MGM movie 'Gaslight')

- Brainwashing
- Convincing someone that they are going insane
- Convincing someone that their understanding of reality is mistaken or false

Hoovers & Hoovering (like a vacuum cleaner, an abuse victim gets 'sucked back in' after leaving or limiting contact with their abuser)

- Outright lies
- Seemingly improved or desirable behavior
- Threats

Denigrate (saying nobody else would ever want/value/have use for you; especially in a relationship)

Constant criticism

Forced activity or skilfully influence in an unfair manner, without regard for a victim's need especially when it is a difficult task for them. There is little or no regard for the victim or others:

Health implication

- E.g. Asking an ill individual to perform tasks that has the potential to harm them further

Physical capability

- E.g. Asked to perform household task like carry extremely heavy objects

Mental capability

- E.g. Asked to work out what is wrong with a person or item that the victim is not trained to

Personal desire or wishes (Forcing a victim to participate in unwanted or uninterested activities, without having a just cause)

- E.g. Forcing a victim to perform or look at sexual acts that are abusive or against their will
- Requiring a victim to care for a parent, child, animal or protect an item, without regard for the victim's wishes or ability
- Using a victim against their will to make a profit

Emotional stress

- To condemn a victim for the abuser's behaviour or the behaviour of others like a child, loved one or pet using:
  - Judgment
  - Blame
  - Shame
  - Guilt

Availability or time required

- E.g. Unreasonable expectations to perform chores or household duties e.g. paint the ceiling or clean a large area in a less than practical time

Use of undue pressure to:

- Sign legal documents
- Not seek legal assistance or advice
- Make beneficiary of their will
- Change a legal will

Jealousy

# Financial or Material Exploitation

- E.g. Cashing the victim's checks without authorization or permission
- Misusing or stealing a victim's money or possessions

Changes in bank account or banking practice,

- Withdrawal of the victim's money
  - Without their permission
  - Forced on the victim

- The Inclusion of additional names on account or signature card

Improper use of power of attorney, conservatorship, or deputyship

- Charging goods to the victim's account
- Abrupt changes in a will or other financial documents
- Unexplained disappearance of funds or valuable possessions;
- Forged signature for financial transactions or for the titles of his/her possessions;

Transfer of assets to from the victim

- The abuser
- Family member
- Someone outside the family

Forcing the victim to take a loan

- For the abuse
- Family member
- Someone outside the family
- The provision of services that are not necessary

# Physical Violence

Occurs when someone uses a part of their body or an object to control or hurt a person. It may result in bodily injury, impairment, physical or mental pain.

## Classifications (UK Law)

Assault

- Common assault (applied unlawful force on the or to make them afraid that immediate force will be used against them)

Battery

- Actual bodily harm (ABH) (harm has been caused but the only intention of the attacker was to assault the victim)
- Grievous bodily harm (GBH) (really serious bodily harm)
  - o Wounding with intent
  - o Wounding without intent

Killing

- Manslaughter (killing the victim without malice aforethought (either express or implied), or in circumstances not amounting to murder)
  - o Voluntary – with intent
  - o Involuntary – without intent
- Murder (where a person of sound mind and discretion unlawfully kills any living being, where the intent was to kill or cause grievous bodily harm)

## Types

Restraints abuse

- Forcible confinement
- Excessive, unwarranted or unnecessary use of physical restraints
- Forcing a person to remain in bed
- Unwarranted use of medication to control a person (aka "chemical restraint")
- Threats with a weapon or object
- Tying the person to a bed or chair

Hair-Pulling

Striking

- With an object
  - o   A vehicle
  - o   Other smaller object
- ▪   e.g. With a hammer, belt, piece of wood, spoon, shoe etc
- Without an object
  - o   Hitting
  - o   Slapping
  - o   Punching

Hurt with feet

- Kicking
- Barefooted
- With shoe
- Stomp

Physical punishment

- Pinching
- Arm-Twisting
- Pushing
- Shoving
- Shaking
- Force-Feeding
- Biting

Medication abuse (Inappropriate use of medication)

- Giving non prescribed medicine to the victim
- Withholding medication
- Medication misuse in care of the victim
  - o   Misuse of prescription
  - o   Overdose
  - o   Under utilization of prescribed drugs

Harm the victim

- Strangling
- Burning
- Stabbing
- Beating
- Choking
- Gouge

Deliberate Exposure

- Severe Weather
- Inappropriate Room Temperatures

Kill the victim

- Accidentally
- Self-defense
- Deliberately
- Premeditative

Burning

- Acid
- Other heat generating liquid
- Flammable fluid
- Burn in localised area
- Set ablaze
- With a hot object

Mark

- Leave a slight bruise

Slam

- To the ground
- Against a wall

Lift

Squeeze

With object

Without an object

Drop

Cut

- With a sharp object
- With a rough object

Throw at the victim

- Object
- Child
- Pet

Throw the victim across the room

Pour or throw substance at the victim

- Liquid
- Powdery substance
- Other types of fluid

Use body fluids or Excrement on the victim

- The victim's
- The abuser's
- Another human being
- Pets

- o Saliva /Spitting
- o Vomit
- o Urine
- o Faeces

Pull or grab

- With hand
- With an object
- Hair pulling
- Finger nails
- Toe nails
- Other parts of your body

Fire arm against the victim

- Shot
- Hit
- Insert
- Gag

Poisoning

May use: Rough treatment, physical abuse or force which results in pain, discomfort, or minor injury, serious injury or death.

Can result in (but not limited to) bruises, black eyes, welts, lacerations, rope marks, bone fractures, broken bones, skull fractures, open wounds, cuts, punctures, cause internal injuries/bleeding, sprains, dislocations etc.

# Sexual Violation and Neglect

Occurs when the victim is unwillingly forced to take part in sexual activity or is violated even though, at the time they are incapable of giving consent.

Touching in a sexual manner without consent

- Kissing
- Grabbing
- Fondling

Forced sexual intercourse

- Rape
- Sodomy

Forcing a person to perform degrading or painful sexual acts

- Beating sexual parts of the body
- unwanted touching

Forcing pornographic material

- View

Participation in pornography

- Sexually explicit photographing
- Filming

Force compliance with:

- Assault
- Battery
    - o   Weapon
    - o   Restraints

Forced prostitution

Exhibitionism or coerced nudity

- Known
- Unknowingly
  - For the abuser
  - For others

Making unwelcome sexual comments

- Jokes
- Leering behaviour
  - In public
- Humiliating
- Criticizing

Neglect

- Withholding sexual affection
- Abuser preferring self gratification but not sexually engaging with the victim
- Adultery

Unwanted practices

- Forced group sex
- Instructed to perform unbecoming acts for their abuser's viewing

Denial of a person's sexuality or privacy (watching);

Denial access to sexual health information

Unfounded allegations

- Promiscuity
- Infidelity

- Inability

Purposefully exposing the victim to sexually transmitted infections

- HIV-AIDS
- Other STD

If while going through this you felt that you can identify with some of the words or phrases, be it as a victim, abuser or both I would advise you to speak to someone. You can start by talking to someone you trust, like a trusted professional, a family member, a confidante, friend or leader, about the situation you find yourself in. If you are a victim I would suggest you get help and make a safety plan. You can also ask for the names of people and places that assist you with coping skills while you are still in the situation. Having said that, the best help, advice and support of victims in any abusive relationship is to leave as quickly and safely as possible. Remember you cannot change anyone but you, so work on your safety, self-confidence and establishing any boundaries in the relationship that you safely can. In addition, once you are out be sure that you get support and help with our healing process.

**Key Principle**

Knowledge truly is the beginning of self-empowerment.

Armed with the information, about the many methods

of abuse, we would know what to look out for

as an abuser is lording over their victim.

# Thank you

I hope you have gleaned a lot from this book and feel a new sense of hope for your future. Armed with knowledge, I want you to take the bold step of reclaiming your life from your abuser and then help others to do the same; someone out there is waiting for you to give them hope.

I have included a list of quick links below. I would be grateful if you can use the first one to go rate this book and give a positive review on Amazon if you found it helpful. This will help make others aware of the book and its value to those who need it.

In addition, please tell others who you believe may benefit, about this book. Share with them what you learnt on Facebook and Twitter. Please do that now as a favour to me, I appreciate it and you will be amazed at the countless others that you will be helping as well. They may be confused or feel stuck and alone in their toxic relationship not knowing where to find the answers or help to get out. Your action can make a difference for them.

Finally, I have included a more extended version Checklist for you to use as a reminder of the things you need to do as you embark on this *Time To Go* journey.

Thank you very much, have a safe transition to your freedom!

Blessings and grateful,


*Norva*

# Resource Page

Use this link to go to my Amazon Author page to rate and review this book:

http://www.amazon.co.uk/Norva-SemoyAbiona/e/B00 UGRE8A0/ref =dp_byline_cont_book_1

Post on our Facebook page at :

https://www.facebook.com/MyChoiceMarriage

Tweet about the book to your followers at:

http://twitter.com use our hashtag #TimeToGoLAR

The checklist - Get a more in depth version :

http://www.TTGTheChecklist.mychoicemarriage.com

For more help, support and information on our other products:

http://www.MyChoiceMarriage.com

For a list of handpicked books on relationship and abusers go to:

http://www.Relationship121.com/Abuse

For free videos on the topic check out our youtube channel:

https://www.youtube.com/channel/UCHv1Utl2sklk8JGO8AQO5_g ?view_as=public

# ABOUT THE AUTHOR

**Norva Semoy Abiona** is a Relationship Coach and Business Owner of Real Fulfilment International. She is well known for the Wise Wife (to enhance your healthy unfulfilling relationship), My Choice Marriage (to help you safely leave your toxic / abusive relationship) and WW Comrade models (to support wives as you implement changes in your life and relationship). As well as being the Author of this book, Norva has written several articles on relationships and a short nonfiction manifesto for wives on the core areas they need to work on improving if they are to enhance their lives and relationships. Some of her work can be found on her website and other related sites. She plans to write another book in the not too distant future, the working title is, 'I'll Go 1st : 13 In-depth Tips on How to Transform Your Marriage Fast By Being a Wise Wife.'

Norva is the Inventor of The Drive Board Game, which is a behaviour awareness tool for young people and adults. She is also an inspirational International Speaker, Wife and Mother. She spent over half a decade working as a trained Community and Family Mediator, Family Group Conference and Restorative Justice Facilitator. Norva is also the owner of www.relationship121.com an online relationship resource and book store.

Norva has successfully faced many adversities during her life, including health issues and escaping an abusive relationship.

In 1994 She got married and quickly found herself in an abusive relationship. After 3 years of hoping and praying for change in her marriage, she briefly mentioned about her situation. Norva then remained tight-lipped for another three years or so but the abuse got even worse and her abuser's strategies more varied. As she puts it, "at the time she was busy planning their wonderful future while ignoring their miserable present."

Early in the year 2000 Norva reached a cross-road in her life. In the preceding 2 years she had focused on her personal development - particularly academically and career-wise. Norva had also given birth a few months prior to her first child. With all that personal growth and changes she came to the realization that what she had been tolerating for all those years was toxic. She was being abused both mentally and physically; now she was wise enough to know that there was a better life out there waiting for her. Norva was wise enough to put aside religious dogma and embrace the Godly principles of happiness, freedom and safety. She made the difficult, and some might say brave, decision to leave her country Trinidad, to get away from the abuse.

Norva migrated to the UK with her then baby daughter in October 2000, where she spent time furthering her studies. Norva also spent time working towards rebuilding her self esteem, self-confidence and providing the best opportunities possible for her daughter.

Soon, Norva became reacquainted with a friend she had met when they were both age 13. They became the best of friends, began courting and after three years got married. She admits that she went into the relationship with a lot of emotional baggage from her past relationship.

Conscious of the need for sustainable change, Norva decided to focus on taking time to improve herself in the area of being a great wife. She began to observe, more than even before, the good things that her husband did and how much they outweighed any difficult issues they had as a couple. Norva focused on the positives, continued her self-development as a woman both spiritually and mentally and she started to treat her husband like a king. It didn't take long for her husband to sit up and take notice. He started paying her more compliments, helping out more and doing those things that she appreciated without her having to ask or prompt. All of that has had such a powerful impact on her life and relationship. Norva went first in freely giving because she believes that it is the best way to give. In return she has been getting over and above her expectations from the relationship.

Norva is passionately dedicated to her husband, family and spiritual growth. She has credited these relationships with helping her beat her battle with cancer and other health issues which she has faced.

Her family stories have been featured in churches and she has been called upon to encourage women with her inspiring stories.

For over a decade she has been sought after for her relationship insights and invaluable advice. Her No Holds Barred and comical straight talk keeps clients and audiences coming back for more. She has helped people with all aspects of relationship support and advice, including from successful matchmaking; which has led to happy marriages, transforming failing marriages, to coping with saying goodbye to a dying spouse. Her speciality is in helping wives start the processes of transforming their failing marriage to one of fulfilment instead of waiting for their husband to change.

Norva is fondly called 'The Relationship Change Catalyst' and 'The Chief Wise Wife.'

Her Mantra is 'Overcome through Change.'

Norva graduated from the University of Westminster with a Masters of Arts merit in Business Studies. She is also an Associate member of the Association of Business Executive through her Advance Diploma in Business Administration.

Norva wants to hear from you. For more information about her books, training programs, products, workshops, etc She can be reached on Facebook, LinkedIn and Twitter @NorvaAbiona.

To book Norva for your next event you can contact her:

Real Fulfilment International

Email: norva@thewisewife.com

Websites: www.TheWiseWife.com

www.MyChoiceMarriage.com